# BOCK

DARRYL RICHMAN

 A Brewers Publications Book

Bock
Darryl Richman
Classic Beer Style Series
Edited by Anne Higman
Technical Edit by Charlie Papazian
Copyright 1994 by Darryl Richman

ISBN 0-937381-39-x
Printed in the United States of America
10 9 8 7 6 5 4 3 2 1

Published by Brewers Publications, Inc.
a division of the Association of Brewers, Inc.
PO Box 1679, Boulder, Colorado 80306-1679 USA
Tel. (303) 447-0816 • FAX (303) 447-2825

Direct all inquiries/orders to the above address.

Cover design by Robert L. Schram
Cover photography foreground by Michael Lichter,
Michael Lichter Photography
Cover photography background by Galen Nathanson
Cover art direction by Marilyn Cohen
Thanks to Rastal GmbH for donating the cover-photo glass

# Table of Contents

# Dedication

I dedicate this book to the fond memory of my grandparents, Joseph and Sarah Tauber, whose love and support are deeply missed.

# Acknowledgments

No man is an island; no book has a single author. I can point to seminal events and associations that have brought me along the steps of this hobby, and which allowed me to lead the authorship of this book. My friend Jeff Clark, a liquor department stock clerk while we were at college, pointed the way. Mike and Nadine Malcolm gave me my first taste of homebrew and allowed me to watch them at work. Kevin Haley and I together brewed my first batch. Ron and Pat Guentzler urged me to take the next steps to mashing and yeast culture. The Maltose Falcons and the Brews Brothers have kept this hobby exciting, fulfilling, and fun for more than seven years.

*Bock* could not have come about without the help and encouragement of the professionals who make the brewing industry a community. I have boundless depths of gratitude for the information and inspiration provided by Dr. George Fix. Professor Dr. Anton Piendl, of the Technical University of Munich in Weihenstephan, set me on the right track in many ways; this book is significantly dependent on his research results. I am indebted

*Bock*

to Bill Siebel for extensive use of his library at the Siebel Institute in Chicago. Herr Inselkammer of Brauerei Aying graciously opened the doors to his brewery and allowed me to pester his brewmaster; Charles Finkel provided the connection and allowed me access to his library. Marty Velas, brewmaster at Southern California Brewing Company of Torrance, California, offered his insight to bock beer.

Randy Mosher, "Dr. Bob Technical", has cast a wide net over the brewing literature and was happy to share his catch. I thank Martin Lodahl for long discussions of homebrewing over the Internet. He would not let me get away with less than my best writing effort. Scribe Bro Rob Nelson helped by reviewing the text and keeping my spirits up. Fritz and Christine Gerneth graciously facilitated my research in Munich.

Elizabeth Gold at Brewers Publications got me into this, and then helped me to get out again. Her patience is immeasurable.

My wife Heather helped translate the German texts that I needed to understand.

All of the recipes were composed on The Brewer's Planner, a recipe formulation and brew logging tool.

# About the Author

Darryl Richman was born and raised in the San Fernando Valley suburbs of Los Angeles, California. He is 36 years old and lives with his wife Heather and their miniature zoo in Bellevue, Washington. He holds a Bachelor of Science degree in Computer Science from California State University at Northridge, and is employed as a computer programmer.

Long a fan of exotic beers from all over the world, his interest in brewing began with an extract-and-grain adjunct batch of beer he helped to brew with his brother- and sister-in-law in 1985. After joining the Maltose Falcons and brewing with extracts, he progressed to yeast cultures and then on to all-grain.

His second batch took a first-place award at a local competition, and he has gone on to win ribbons in many competitions in the West. He has won first-place awards at both the AHA and the HWBTA national competitions and at the Dixie Cup super regional.

Since passing the BJCP exam in 1988, he has attained the National Judge level. Active in helping others learn to judge, he proctors exams and gives preparatory classes.

He wrote for, and eventually became editor of, *Brews & News*, the Maltose Falcons' monthly newsletter. His articles have also been published in the pages of **zymurgy**, *Beer and Brewing* series books, *Brewing Techniques*, and *The Celebrator*.

He has developed a number of computer-based brewing aids, and is currently president of The Crafty Fox, which develops and sells The Brewer's Planner, a recipe formulation and batch logging tool.

Besides beer and companionship, Darryl enjoys riding his motorcycle, playing racquetball, hiking, and computer hacking.

# Introduction

I didn't enjoy my first taste of Bock beer ...

I distinctly remember how my friend Jeff asked me and our circle of friends to help him develop his beer bottle collection. Having recently come of age, we happily complied, taking an interest in all of the strange, imported beers that we were newly allowed to purchase. Most of them were variants on the familiar Pilsener theme, some more sweet and some more bitter. One of the bottles that happened to come my way was EKU 28, certainly one of the most potent beers available. Being young and foolish, I poured this beer out and took a healthy slug. The results were as predictable as they were unpleasant. I looked over the label, reading it carefully, so that I could avoid this kind of beer in the future.

I soon discovered, however, that this wasn't the only kind of Bock beer available. One sunny spring day, my roommates came home from the supermarket with their newest find — Pabst Bock.

We had already discarded the oxymoron, *good American beer*. The concepts *American industrial brew* and *a strong, thick beer*, did not intersect in my mind. I was fairly perplexed, and somewhat intrigued, to see that one of the giants was putting out something like that strange stuff I had first tried.

It turned out that Pabst Bock was not like the EKU, except perhaps in color. It seemed to be just another marketing gimmick — it was much like their standard product, colored dark and a bit sweeter. Still, one had to admit that the caramel color and flavor lent more interest to the regular Pabst, and now it seemed evident that Bock beer must have a range, from sweet and watery to huge and cloying. I figured there must be some middle ground in there that I could appreciate. No longer afraid of the appellation, I cautiously set out on the road to trying various beers.

Bock beer has had a long, and generally unexplored history. It has traveled about a bit, and has changed considerably since its origins in the 13th century. It has had moments of celebration and centuries of fame.

The Germans have codified Bock and Doppelbock into their law, as subtypes of *starkbier* ("strong beer"). Until recently, any beer intended for sale in the German market had to be brewed according to the Reinheitsgebot (the famous Beer Purity law). In 1989 though, a Common Market Court declared that Germany could not use the law to keep out non-conforming beers from other Common Market countries. As a result, countries belonging to the Common Market can sell beers in Germany without complying with the purity law. German brewers and countries not belonging to the Common Market, however, must continue to comply. The Reinheitsgebot states that beer must be made from the classic four ingredients: malted barley or wheat, hops, water, and yeast. (Exceptions are made for processing agents like water salts.)

This scene depicts the luxuries of life: good food and drink, a fine cigar, music, and stimulation for the mind. Photo by Klaus Koch.

A Bock must be brewed from a wort of at least 1.064 (16 °Plato), and a Doppelbock from at least 1.072 (18 °Plato). The German government has turned these styles into labeling laws, related to standardized beer strength levels (based on attenuation from starting gravity). Any beer in these ranges qualifies for the title.

In other countries, no such restrictions hold. Bock-style beers are now produced in many variations around the world, though they may not always be labeled as Bock beer. I have sampled interesting examples from Italy and South America. Look for beers advertising *Doppio-Malto*, for example, and see if you don't agree that these are Bock-style beers.

Beers labeled as Bock don't necessarily fit into the traditional mold. The American interpretation is probably the prime example of this.[1, 2] As far back as the repeal of Prohibition, brewers in the United States were more concerned about introducing their Bock beers on the same day than with producing a beer that resembled the original style. By 1937, the *Brewer's Technical Review*[3,4] announced that the major breweries had finally, after several years' negotiation, all agreed to introduce their spring Bock beers on the evening of March 16th — just in time for St. Patrick's day: quite a change for a beer that had been introduced on the day of St. Joseph in Munich for several centuries.

Microbreweries and brewpubs represent a reversal in the trend toward brewery consolidation on the North American continent, generating a return to more faithful interpretations of the style. There are now many interesting Bocks produced by these small brewers, in all of the variations that Bock beer has seen through the ages: Maibocks, Doppelbocks, Helles Bocks, Bocks brewed with ale yeast, and even an Eisbock.

I hope this guide can provide historical insight to the development of this beer style over seven centuries of change. I include discussion of the modern styles of Helles Bock and Maibock, and how they developed from the Dunklesbock style, and Doppelbock. Weizenbock, a strong, dark, wheat beer more closely allied with

Weizenbier (and discussed more fully in *German Wheat Beer* by Eric Warner),[5] is only mentioned briefly.

I have sought to lay out recipes, techniques, and procedures for home and small scale brewers, useful for the creation of these beers in the historic and modern styles. I have tried to produce recipes for authentic tasting beers, in so far as comparisons were possible. Where that was not feasible, I undertook to emulate materials and procedures as closely as I could interpret the written records, hoping to reproduce historic styles.

Originally I was concerned that there would not be enough material to write a book; now I appreciate the number and variety of sources available. I hope I've provided a clear, coherent, and concise description of this billy-goat's tale.

# 1

# The History of Bock Beer

## OHNE EINBECK GÄBS KEIN BOCKBIER

"Without Einbeck, there would be no Bock Beer" —
advertising slogan for Einbecker Brauhaus AG, the last
remaining brewery in Einbeck.

The origins of this story are widely perceived to be
in the small town of Einbeck, located in what is today
the northern German state of Lower Saxony
*(Niedersachsen)*. We first hear about the rise of Einbeck,
or Eimbeck, or Eimbock, as documents of the time have
variously spelled it, in the 13th century, during the
Middle Ages.

The medieval period was a time of social fragmenta-
tion and strife. After the fall of the Roman Empire, feu-
dalism became the political rule. Europe was shattered
into many small kingdoms and duchies. Political power
was in constant flux between the Papacy, the German
Emperor (heir to the Holy Roman Empire), kings,
princes, dukes (German as well as French, Danish,
Italian, and Swedish), and free cities. Whenever it

appeared that one political force would reach a position of dominance, one or more of the others would cooperate just long enough to tear it back down.

Free cities evolved as a result of placing their support behind some other faction, who, upon winning a battle, granted them a charter. They became regional centers of commerce, for that was their strength. They were most prevalent at the further reaches of the Holy Roman Empire, where the Pope or the German Emperor had less influence.

Bremen, Lübeck, and Hamburg were perhaps the largest of the free cities in the North. The former two, located on either side of the Danish peninsula, over time developed a brisk merchant trade between them, connecting the Baltic with the North seas. However, as the Danes proved fierce raiders, these merchants united to protect the road between them. This confederation, or *hanse*, grew into a large loosely held trading association known as the Hanseatic League.

The League was formed to protect each city's economic interests. Together they grew to control all trade through the North and Baltic seas. The league occasionally raised armies and navies to fight off invaders, subdue pirates, or take other lands into their control. They built trade houses in a number of foreign trading ports, and dealt with foreign governments to secure exclusive trading rights. At its height the League included over 80 cities, all of them led by the city of Lübeck.

One of the specialties of many of the Hansa cities was their beers, which were highly regarded, commanding a premium price far and wide.

The freedom to brew for sale was not a widespread privilege in medieval times. The church or nobility reserved this right to themselves, granting it to others

This was the official trade entrance gate to the medieval free city of Lübeck. Photo by Darryl Richman.

only when it suited them. Usually such a grant was made when the authorities grew tired or unable to brew themselves, and then only in exchange for the taxes that could be raised by dint of the brewer's craft.

Whenever the right to brew was granted to a city, a brewers' guild would spring up to regulate what was brewed, and when, and how much was to be made by each brewer. In times of poor harvest (and therefore, high priced grain), the guild might specify how much the brewer could dilute the product. Guilds would often have a strong say in what ingredients were used and how the brewer made his beer. While this was an infringement, the guilds generally prevented the government from involving itself in the brewers' business by participating in city politics.

This was the typical state of affairs in the Hansa cities. It was good business: the taxes made the nobles,

the church, or the cities rich, while the guilds made the brewers rich.

Each city's beer had its own character and was praised for its features. Historic records show that some beers were well regarded for their nutritional character, others for medicinal purposes, and note was taken of each beer's alcoholic strength.

It is not surprising to find that in those days beer was considered both food and medicine, and not just a social drink. With the brewing materials and methods of the time, the beer was usually cloudy and sweet. This came from the high protein and starch levels carried over from unmalted grains and poorly mashed and lautered malts. From such a drink substantial food value in the form of carbohydrates, protein, and vitamins was available in an easily assimilable form. It was embraced for its healthy qualities and it raised the spirits — all the same attributes as chicken soup, and it also kept better.

## BIERSTADT EINBECK*

*\*Text appearing on three oak casks that grace the
entrance to the city of Einbeck.*

Einbeck began as an estate held by nobles living in the great Hansa city of Hamburg. It grew to a small town, and eventually was given a charter as a city sometime between 1203 and 1256. By then, Einbeck had grown large enough to join the League.[6]

Records of hop cultivation in Germany date from 822 AD, but the first written mention of their being added to beer does not occur until the publication of Saint Hildegard von Bingen's *Physica Sacra* (1150-1160).

*Gruit,* a generic term for proprietary combinations of bittering and flavoring herbs, was commonly used in beer to cut the sweet flavor and add medicinal value. Such mixtures might include ash leaves, myrtle bark, rosemary, or sweet gale. Many a bishopric was floated on the taxes obtained, and many families became rich on the profits from a successful gruit recipe held close to the vest. Even today the recipes for a number of patent cordials and soft drinks, such as Coca Cola and Dr. Pepper, are closely held secrets and continue to reap profits for their owners.

This stained glass in the Einbecker Brauhaus brewery emphasizes the traditional aspects of the German brewing industry. The wooden mash tun is surmounted by the trademarked crowned E device, with a hop cone, an ear of barleycorns, a malt shovel, and a sampling bucket. The couplet, a touchstone in Germany, loosely translates as "God save the hops and malt". Photo by Darryl Richman.

Einbeck had the fortune to be founded in a center of hop gardening just when hop usage was first blossoming in Germany, and in a place not under the control of the Church. This latter aspect meant that there was no taxing authority to demand the use of gruit, which, combined with the ready supply of fresh hops, undoubtedly aided the flavor of the Einbeck product. It may also have helped the beer to remain stable throughout the time it took to transport it.

Over the next century, Einbeck became a renowned brewing center, outstripping the fame of its larger neighbors in the League. By 1385, there were 600 private houses brewing Einbecker beer within the city. The city's mayor was also its chief brewmaster. The citizen-brewers worked in a cooperative fashion, with the brewmaster producing a wort for each of them, and they in turn tending to the fermentation.[7] The city subsequently purchased the output from the private houses, blended the beer, and then warehoused and brokered the beer. The trademark crowned-E device was owned by the city; none of the private brewers were allowed to use it separately.

Einbeck's brewing prowess grew to the point that its beer was exported across the Baltic Sea to Russia, Sweden, and Denmark; and across the North Sea to Belgium, the Netherlands, France, and England. From there, it was also carried by Venetian boats into the Mediterranean. Overland, it was transported throughout the Holy Roman Empire. It is written that Einbecker beer was exported as far away as Jerusalem. Many of the Hansa port cities had depots specifically constructed for Einbecker beer, so regular and frequent was the trade.

A writer of the time, Jacobus Theodorus Tabernaemontanus, in 1613 cataloged a list of the exact attributes of many of the Hansa cities' beers, their flavors, aromas, and uses. This was how he described Einbeck's beer: "thin, subtle, clear, of bitter taste, has a pleasant acidity on the tongue, and many other good qualities."[6]

The crowned-E trademark of Einbeck is still in use today. Label is from the collection of Charles Finkel.

Other records indicate that the famous Einbecker beer was composed of one-third wheat malt and two-thirds barley malt, all of the palest color available. It was clearly brewed as an ale, but only during the winter (from St. Martin's Day at the end of September through the first of May), so that it may have been lagered, or cold conditioned, as Alt beer is today. Such a process would certainly add to the beer's stability.

Einbeck maintained its position as a premier brewing center through the 14th and 15th centuries. Its beer grew in fame, and was frequently a part of lavish gifts. Martin Luther received a present of Einbecker beer on the occasion of his wedding.[8] He was also sustained at the Diet of Worms in 1521 on a cask given to him by Duke Erich of Brunswick, since he had given up solid food for Lent. His success at that ordeal, combined with his personal endorsement of the beer, added to the fame of Einbeck.

Early in the 17th century, however, the Thirty Years' War, combined with the appearance of other free cities in Holland and Poland, the increasingly hostile Danish and Swedish Kingdoms, and the rise of Prussia, eventually brought down the Hanseatic League, and Einbeck with it. The northern trade routes, so long monopolized by the League through its ports, were disrupted, and the financial might of the cities was drained. In 1669, only Lübeck, Bremen, and Hanover were left to officially dissolve the League.

With the demise of the League, Einbeck's exports dropped and distribution was confined to Northern Germany. In 1650, a fire wiped out much of Einbeck, including its brewery. A new brewery was constructed, but it burned down as well, and was eventually replaced by two separate breweries. Over time, these came into private hands and became competing operations. In the 1920s they merged to form Einbecker Brauhaus, which is now the only brewing concern in Einbeck. Since 1972 it has been a satellite in the Dortmunder Union-Schultheiß AG system.[7] Today it produces over 500,000 barrels (600,000 hL) of beer, and nearly a quarter of that output is the strong beer that made Einbeck famous.

## MEANWHILE, IN MUNICH . . .

While the world's oldest continuously operating brewery is Weihenstephan in Bavaria, brewing was not nearly so advanced in the South. Weihenstephan was founded as early as 1040, but commercial brewing took another 200 years to start, and it was the middle of the 14th century before it began to become important.

Bavaria knew of the fame and flavor of the beers from the north, as they were brought overland to the Munich nobility at the end of the 15th century.[9] They were very well received and may have inspired the famous *Reinheitsgebot*, or Beer Purity Law, which began as a local Munich ordinance in 1487. The law was enlarged to cover all of Bavaria in 1516 by Duke Wilhelm IV, as an attempt to increase the quality of the local beer. At this time, official beer tasters were appointed. Their duty was to verify the quality of each brewer's product, thrice per week in the summer and twice in the winter.

For years local brewing talents continued to be meager. In an effort to produce a reasonable drink, Duke Ludwig X brought a Brunswick brewmaster to Munich in 1540 for the express purpose of reproducing the strong beer of the North.[10] Also in 1540, Einbeck set up a depot in Landshut, a short day's journey from Munich, and five years later, another in Munich itself.[9] Eventually,

## Der Vierd tail.

d.18 süllb den pfarrern in vnserm Lande nit gestatt werdñ
sol/außgenomen was die pfarrer vnd geystlichen von aigñ
weinwachsen haben/vnd für sich/ir pfarrgesellen /priester
schafft vnnd hausgesund/auch in der not den kindlpetterin
vnd krancken leüten/ vnuirlich geben/ das mag ine gestat
werden. Doch geuirlicher weyp/von schenckhens vnd ge-
wins wegen/söllen sy kainen wein einlegen.

### Wie das pier summer vñ winter auf dem Land sol geschenckt vnd prauen werden

Item Wir ordnen/setzen/vnnd wöllen/ mit Rathe vnn'er
Lanndtschafft / das für an allennthalben in dem Fürsten-
thumb Bayrñ/auff dem lande/ auch in vnsern Stetten vñ
Märckthen/da derhalb hieuor kain sonndere ordnung ist/
von Michaelis biß auff Georj / ain maß oder kopff piers
über ainen pfenning Müncher werung/vñ von sant Je-
gen tag/biß auff Michaelis / die maß über zwen pfenning
derselben werung / vnd der enden der kopff ist / über drey
haller/bey nachgesetzter Pene/nicht gegeben noch auf ge-
schenckht sol werden. Wo auch ainer nit Merrzñ / sonder
annder Pier prawen/oder sonst haben würde/sol Er doch
das/Eains wegs höher/dann die maß vmb ainen pfenning
schencken/vnd verkauffen. Wir wöllen auch sonderlichen/
das für an allenthalben in vnsern Stetten/Märckthen/vñ
auff dem Lannde/zu kainem Pier/ merer stückh/dañ al-
lain Gersten /Hopffen/vñ wasser/genomen vñ gepraucht
sölle werdñ. Welher aber dise vnsere Ordnung wissendlich
überfaren vnnd nit hallten wurde / dem sol von seiner ge-
richtsöbrigkait / dasselbig vas Pier/ zustraff vnnachläß-
lich/ so offt es geschicht / genomen werden. Jedoch wo
ain Gastwirt von ainem Pierprewen in vnsern Stettñ/
Märckten/oder auf in lande/ yezuzeitñ ainen Emer piers/

The Text of the Reinheitsgebot of 1516 displaying the Bayrische dialect. With this document, Duke Wilhelm IV decreed that pure beer was every-one's right in Bavaria. Photo by Klaus Koch.

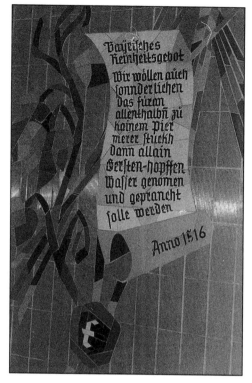

The Einbecker beer came south to Bavaria, and the Reinheitsgebot returned north. This mosaic of hops and barley behind a decree labled Bavarian Reinheitsgebot is set in the wall of the brew house at Einbeck. Photo by Darryl Richman.

under the reign of Wilhelm V, the royal court brewery — the Hofbräuhaus München — was constructed and completed on All Saints' Day, 1589.

In the beginning of the 17th century, with the decline of the Hanseatic League already well under way, Munich breweries began to produce credible imitations of the northern beers. The Reformation and Counter-Reformation created deep divisions between the Catholic south and Protestant north, and that, combined with the high cost of overland transportation, caused Bavaria to be even more isolated from the North than in the previous century. With little hope of obtaining the imported beers, the Münchners were forced to make their own.

At the time, Munich made two general styles of beer, Braunbier and Weißbier. Braunbier was an all-barley malt beer, brown with red highlights. The original Hofbräuhaus became known as the Old Brown Brewery and a second brewery was built in 1602, called the White Brewery, reflecting which types of beer were made in each. Weißbier was a sour wheat beer that today we more closely associate with Berlin.

In 1612, Duke Maximillian I persuaded the brewmaster of Einbeck, Elias Pichler, to come to Munich.[11,12] Once in Munich, the brewmaster was not allowed to leave the town, so valuable were his skills considered.[12] Two years later, in 1614, the Hofbräuhaus introduced its version of the Einbecker beer, brewed at the Brown Brewery. In 1638 the strong beer was released to the general public. It was instantly popular, and required the brewery to be expanded several times to make up for the displaced brown beer production.

## A BEER BY ANY OTHER NAME

The careful reader may have noticed that this narrative has so far refrained from actually using the term *Bock beer*. This is because there are a number of different theories about its origin.

One theory asserts that the beer was only produced under the sign of Capricorn the goat — *Bock* being the German word for billy-goat — in late December and January. This seems least credible since the beer was produced whenever feasible.

Another links an old German word, *Pogkmedt*, meaning mead, to the Bock beer that rivaled it in strength.[13] From there, through corruption and contraction of pronunciation, came *Bock*.

The most widely accepted belief is that the name comes from the corruption of the Einbeck name. In the Bavarian dialect of German, called *Bayrische*, the locally produced imitation of the fine beer imported from the North was called *Ainpoeckische*.[11,9] The Bavarian predilection for the hard 'P' sound in preference to the softer 'B' extended to the word beer as well, consequently known as "Pier" (one can see it spelled as "Pier" in the text of the Reinheitsgebot). We may reasonably believe that this was shortened to *Poeckishe Pier* or just *Poeckpier* (Bock beer).

A more fanciful explanation for the name, and the one I enjoy most as a cautionary tale on the dangers of drinking to excess, is this one from *One Hundred Years of Brewing*:[14]

"There is probably no fact, in connection with the history of brewing, about which more has been written and a greater number of explanations offered than as to the origin of Bock-beer. One of the latest and best gives the honor to a medieval knight of Brunswick, who, having cast aspersions upon the beer offered him by Duke Christoph of Bavaria, was challenged by the enraged brewmaster to a formal drinking bout. Upon the day of the contest, the castle of the Bavarian lord was beautifully decorated and the ladies of the court were present in great numbers to witness the outcome. Suddenly the band, which had been discoursing martial airs, stopped, and a keg of Brunswick beer and one of Bavaria were placed side by side. The brewmaster drank from the Brunswick keg and the Brunswick knight from that of Bavaria, two immense vessels, holding more than two gallons each, being the bumpers. Each drained his gigantic cup, the gentleman from Brunswick still making sarcastic remarks about the strength of the court beer of

*Bock*

The Müchner Kindl, the symbol of the city of Munich.
Photo by Darryl Richman.

Munich.

"The brewmaster, however, was confident that his opponent would finally succumb, despite his bold front, and, as he handed him the second cup, said: 'Now we will empty another to your health, and, in half an hour, the one who can thread a needle while standing on one foot, shall be declared the winner.'

"When the vessels had been again emptied, a maid was sent for needles and thread and, returning, carelessly left open the gate of the court-yard. At the very moment that each contestant was preparing to stand on one leg and attempt his task, a pet goat frisked into the yard. The Bavarian brewmaster succeeded in threading his needle, while the Brunswick knight dropped his three times and concluded by falling and rolling on the pavement, claiming that the *'Bock'* had thrown him. Duke Christoph and his court were convulsed with laughter, remarking, 'The Bock that threw you over was brewed by me.'"

Some basis in fact for this story can be sought in history, because Brunswick is a Saxon neighbor of Einbeck, and the Duke's daughter married a knight from Brunswick in a ceremony held in Munich. Or perhaps this story is merely an allegory of the larger rivalry between the North and the South, the Hohenzollern and the Wittelsbach, the Protestant and the Catholic, the pale beer and the brown.

Regardless of how the Bock name was chosen, one thing is certain: it was chosen in Munich. As the brown beer was Munich's staple malt beer, Bock beer was founded on this base.

## THE ORIGINS OF DOPPELBOCK

While Bock beer originated in northern Germany and migrated south, Doppelbock is a home-grown style. It sprang not from commercial brewing as with Einbeck, but from the monastic brewers for which the city of Munich got its name (*München,* the native spelling, means "home of the monks").

While the nobility could afford to purchase the beer they liked, the monks relied on beer to fulfill basic needs. Beer was more than a pleasant drink: it was an important source of potable water and nutrients. Naturally, they took up the art and science of brewing, in an age when such information was difficult to come by.

Followers of St. Francis of Paula came to Munich from Italy during the Counter-Reformation to help maintain Catholicism in Bavaria,[7,8,9] bringing their rites and beliefs, including vegetarianism, with them. The calendar played an important part in daily monastic life, dictating what was brewed. Twice annually Paulaners fasted for extended periods: the forty days of Lent leading up to Easter, and the four weeks of Advent preceding Christmas.

During these fasts, no solid food was allowed.

However, liquids were not restricted, including beer. The oft-repeated nickname "liquid bread" was literally true, as the brewers of Paulaner worked hard to brew the most nutritious beer they could for these times. They produced a strong, rich beer that has come down through the ages to us as *Salvator*, now made in the commercial Paulaner brewery.

As with Bock, there is controversy over the origin of the name Salvator, but the choices are more limited.[9] One side claims that the name comes from a phrase in the benediction which asks for the blessings of the Holy Father (" ...ad sanctum Salvatorem"). This is supported by the fact that the beer hall opened by the brothers during the reign of Duke Albrecht V was named the *Salvatorkeller*.

Another argument holds that the beer was originally named Saintly Father Beer (*Sankt-Vater-Bier*) because of the nutrition and joy it provided during the hard times of fasting. After evolving to appeal to the public, who were allowed to buy the beer beginning in 1780,[8] it gradually changed to the Salvator we know today. The name was definitely fixed by 1850.

This beer evolved naturally along a completely different line from Bock beer. It was the Munich public that began calling the beer a double Bock, noting that it was stronger and more nutritious than even the Hofbräuhaus' Bock beer. One thing is clear about the name: it was not called a Doppelbock beer until relatively recently.

In the first decade of the 19th century, all of the monasteries were secularized by Napoleon. The Bavarian Wittelsbachs either leased or sold the breweries to private parties and taxed them to raise revenue. The Paulaner brewery came into the hands of the Zacherl family,[9] and for much of the 1800s its output was not identified with the Paulaner name, although the reputation of the Salvator beer was widespread.

It began to be imitated by other commercial brewers who were jealous of the fame and envious of the sales of the strong beer. In homage to the original, or perhaps trying to ride Salvator's coattails, many gave names to their beers that included the *-ator* suffix.

Since the time of secularization, the purpose for these beers has changed from a necessity to a luxury. The nature of the beer has changed as well. Historical records[2,15,16,17,18,19,20] show that over the last 150 years the original gravity of Doppelbocks has not changed much, but the final gravity has continually decreased; hence, the alcohol level has increased.

For example, Salvator beer from the 1850s, brewed with an original gravity of 1.074 (18.5 °Plato) had a terminal gravity of 1.034 (8.5 °Plato). This yields an alcohol level of about 4.2 percent w/v (5.3 percent v/v). Today,

Paulaner dray wagon with beer barrels. Photo by Darryl Richman.

Early in December, each year, the Ayinger brewery celebrates the availability of its Weihnacts-Bock (Christmas Bock) by ceremoniously tapping the first barrel at the Platzl in Munich. Photo by Darryl Richman.

Salvator, with an identical starting gravity, has an alcohol level of 6.1 percent w/v (7.7 percent v/v).

Also, while the beer was originally devised for use at different, specific times of the year, Doppelbocks in general, and Salvator in particular, are now associated with St. Joseph's day (the 19th of March).[8] On that day, there is a special tapping ceremony for Salvator at Munich's Frühjahrs-Starkbier-Festes ("spring strong beer fest"), and Doppelbocks are widely drunk into April, when Dunkles (dark) and Helles (pale) Bocks take the baton, which is subsequently passed along on the first of May, when Maibocks come into season.[21]

Bocks and Doppelbocks are also popular all through the fall, winter and spring, when they provide the extra *Gemütlichkeit* needed to endure cold, short, gray days.

# 2

# Bock and Doppelbock
# Beer Profiles

Beer styles are not specified and engineered before-hand. They evolve naturally according to local tastes, materials, and resources. Only after the fact are they recognized by brewers, drinkers, and sometimes, governments as official styles. As with any other beer "style", there can be no hard rules. Brewmasters (and sometimes accountants and marketers) will have their way and name their beers as they please. No style statement can be both completely comprehensive and definitive.

Before continuing the discussion of Bock and Doppelbock profiles, a review of flavor characteristics is appropriate and allows for a more thorough understanding of the subject matter. The concept of a primary, secondary, or tertiary flavor characteristic is from *Principles of Brewing Science*,[22] which is an approximation of work done by Meilgaard and reported in *Malting and Brewing Science*.[23] The idea is that a primary flavor is one that exists in beer at more than twice its sensory threshold. A secondary flavor appears at from one half to two times its threshold, and a tertiary flavor is below one half of the threshold level. Primary flavors are significant contributors to the total character of the beer; secondary flavors contribute background notes; and tertiary flavors do not, of themselves, contribute, although it is possible that there can be perceptible synergistic effects.

Anyone who has tried one of the Munich members of this family knows that beers in the Bock style are malty. They have a strong malt aroma when fresh, are big and chewy, with a sweetness up front in proportion to their rich body. A Helles Bock or Maibock will have more emphasis in the fresh malty flavors, while Dunkles Bocks and Doppelbocks will include some darker caramel, and occasionally smoky or chocolatey flavors thrown in.

In lesser versions, there may be some husky astringency that will mar the smooth, rich maltiness. This may happen when the brewer is working too hard to get the last bit of extract from what is, by its nature, an expensive beer to make. The maltiness is not done to the exclusion of other flavors, however; these beers possess balance.

*Balance* is a peculiar word in beer tasting, and especially so for Bock, which is inherently at one end of the taste spectrum, heavy in malt.

The key to understanding balance in this context is to realize that even though the hop aromas and flavors will definitely be on the light side, they will still not be found wanting. The hopping rate is crucial! Without the skeleton of hop bitterness to give shape to the beer, it would turn out very flabby and unappetizing indeed. This bitterness is not so much a primary taste characteristic as it is a foil to allow the palate to appreciate the best points of the malt flavor. This sort of balance keeps the palate from quickly growing tired. It shows up greatest in the aftertaste, which in a well-made Bock is long and lingering, and surprisingly dry. This requirement for balance is especially true of the Doppelbocks, without which they would have to be sipped like liqueurs.

Another sensation that appears in Bock beers, of course, is ethanol. It provides a warmth to ward off the winter chill and adds some sweetness. These are primary flavor characteristics. However, these must be in balance with the malt and hop character of the beer. A German brewmaster told me that the secret to producing a fine Doppelbock is that the drinker should be able to appreciate the product as a great beer first, only realizing the strength when getting up from the table. Although the alcohol content of Bock beers has been rising over the last century, it is still unusual for the alcoholic warmth and sweetish flavor to compete with, rather than support the malt and hop flavors.

Furthermore, the harsh aromas and flavors of fusel oils, or higher (longer chained) alcohols, are definitely not appreciated. The only way to rein in the production of higher alcohols from the high gravity worts that Bocks and Doppelbocks require is through careful control of the fermentation process.

This same control, combined with careful attention to preventing oxidation, will also keep down the production of unwanted aldehydes and esters. The cold temperatures will slow the yeast down, forcing it to take its time at the huge banquet that a high gravity wort presents. This will prevent the yeast from running wild through any one particular biochemical pathway where it might otherwise be inclined to indulge because of the overabundance of malt sugars and nutrients.

## ALTES BOCK

The prefix *Alt* means old, old style or old-fashioned, and is used to imply that the item is created in the original or old-time way. Unfortunately, there is not enough detailed information to know that we have really brewed the Salvator of the 1780s, the Ainpoeckisches Pier of 1614, or the Einbecker Bier of the 1300s. The difficulty in producing old-fashioned beers is that the techniques used are unclear; the actual barley, hops, and wheat strains are unknown and unavailable; the yeasts are unobtainable; and the accompanying microflora indeterminate. Furthermore, peoples' tastes change. What was "pleasant acidity" in the middle ages may be rather sour today. In total, the task seems pretty daunting.

We know that hard-won brewing gains were considered trade secrets passed on only through apprenticeship, never written down where prying eyes might find them. I have read accounts of the Einbecker brewmaster who moved south to Munich which imply that he was a traitor to his city.

Therefore the style descriptions provided are very rough. I have added question marks to parameters that can only be estimated. All of the numbers are broad ranges, reflecting that none of these measurements were available to brewers in these times, so even if they had wanted to communicate them to others, they would have been unable to do so in an objective fashion.

Since we cannot compare our results directly, technique may not matter much. The grist would have been stone ground, rather coarsely; a Corona-type flour mill set rather loosely may be a good approximation. Sometimes the false bottom in the mash/lauter tun was created by placing straw in the vessel (which would have been constructed of wood) and then adding the mash on top of it. Some older brewing texts suggest a mashing protocol of alternating boiling and blood temperature water, with drainings in between. This is sometimes distinguished with the first one or two runnings being used for the highest quality beer, and subsequent runnings used for one or two lesser beers.[19]

## MITTELALTER EINBECKER BIER

Original Gravity: 1.060-1.070 (15-17.5 °Plato)
Final Gravity: 1.020-1.025 (5-6.25 °Plato)
Apparent Degree of Attenuation: 65-70 percent
Real Degree of Attenuation: 52-56 percent
Alcohol Content: 4.0-4.5 percent w/v (5-5.7 percent v/v)
pH: 3.0-3.5 (?)
Bitterness: 40-60 IBU (?)
Color: 10-14 °SRM (25-35 °EBC) (?)

This beer was made from a grist of one-third wheat malt and two-third barley malt, using the palest malts available. Most beer of the time was very dark brown or black, because there was little control over the malting and kilning process. The color here indicated is a bit darker than modern English Pale Ales, which although they are amber in color, got that name because they were the palest beers of their time. I've added some more color since we are looking back several more centuries.

The yeast used was wild, but selected; barrels that produced bad beer were destroyed, and good ones reused.[13] It was undoubtedly a mixed culture of *Saccharomyces cerevisiae* and other *Saccharomyces* species, probably including *Brettanomyces* species and bacteria. In

*31*

such circumstances, the yeast would be very under-atten-
uating by modern standards, and the resulting beer
would have much more body and sweetness than a beer
of today. (More information on mixed cultures is available in Guinard's *Lambic*.)[24]

Modern mashing and lautering techniques were
unknown, so it is likely that a great deal of unreduced
starch and protein was carried over into the boil and
subsequent fermentation. This would produce higher
gravities, but would not add to the sweetness of the beer.

The beer was only produced during the cold part of
the year, and was consumed within a few months of the
end of fermentation, so some of the more fastidious
organisms would not have had a chance to work. This,
along with the testimony of Tabernaemontanus, leads to
the conclusion that the beer had a noticeable, but not
strong, acidity.

Einbeck is situated at the headwaters of the
tributaries of the Leine river and surrounded by
mountains. Its water is very soft snow melt. This water
does not travel very far, and it is all above ground, so we
can assume that it would not pick up any mineral
hardness.[25] Thus the water may be similar in character to
that of Pilsen.

Hops are no longer grown in the region, but we can
assume that they were low alpha varieties. (They were *all*
low alpha varieties in the past, before modern intensive
breeding programs were undertaken). We cannot tell
how the hops were handled, or what drying techniques
— if any — were used. Because it was not yet understood
what part of the hop flower was important to brewing,
the female plants would not have been segregated, and
the resulting hops would have had an even lower alpha
acid rating because of the additional weight of the hop

seeds. The effective alpha acid levels must have been very low indeed.

Since Einbeck often falls below freezing during the winter and all beer was brewed from fall through spring, the implication is that the hops would have been relatively fresh. The hopping rate must have been very high to counter the sweetness of the under-attenuated beer, and also to keep the non-*Saccharomyces* organisms at bay. (This might work out to approximately 4 to 5.5 ounces of a modern 3 percent alpha acid variety per five- gallon batch.)

## AINPOECKISCHES PIER

Original Gravity: 1.060-1.070 (15-17.5 °Plato)
Final Gravity: 1.020-1.025 (5-6.25 °Plato)
Apparent Degree of Attenuation: 62-68 percent
Real Degree of Attenuation: 50-55 percent
Alcohol Content: 4.2-4.7 percent w/v (5.2-5.9 percent v/v)
pH: 3.4-3.8 (?)
Bitterness: 25-40 IBUs (?)
Color: 15-25 °SRM (40-65 °EBC) (?)

This Bock beer was produced by the Hofbräuhaus München after they obtained the secrets of brewing used in Einbeck.

The beer was made from an all-barley malt mash, as the Reinheitsgebot had already long been the law of the land. To complicate things further, although the brewmaster from the North would have wanted to specify pale malts, that would not have proven feasible. The water in the Isar River that flows through Munich is a chalky green color, and contains a lot of carbonates — at least 150 mg/L, while 50 mg/L is often quoted as an upper limit for mashes of pale malts.[22] It would not have been possible to obtain conversion and the relatively clear beer that the Duke required with that combination. The Munich brewers already knew that, and had overcome the problem with the use of acidifying darker malts.

Munich is also not in the center of a hop growing region, although there is a lot of hop cultivation done to the north around the town of Spalt, to the northeast in the Hallertau region just beyond Nürnberg near Hersbruck, and to the west around the town of Tettnang near the *Bodensee* (Lake Constance). The overland distances involved would have made hops a more precious ingredient, and the prodigious hopping rate would have been cut back. Also the Munich brewmasters knew that a lower rate produced a more balanced beer with their darker malts and reduced the harsh character that the carbonates in the water elicited from the hops.

As this beer was brewed for local, and therefore quicker consumption with less handling involved, there must have been an even smaller chance for the competing organisms to gain a foothold. Thus, this beer was probably less acidic than its northern cousin.

## SANKT-VATER-BIER

Original Gravity: 1.075-1.085 (18-20.5 °Plato)
Final Gravity: 1.030-1.035 (7.5-9 °Plato)
Apparent Degree of Attenuation: 60-65 percent
Real Degree of Attenuation: 48-52 percent
Alcohol Content: 4.5-5.5 percent w/v (5.6-6.9 percent v/v)
pH: 3.6-4.2 (?)
Bitterness: 25-35 IBUs (?)
Color: 25-35 °SRM (65-90 °EBC) (?)

This beer was originally brewed by the brothers of Saint Francis from the Italian city of Paula for their own consumption during times of fasting. It was intended as a nutrient substitute for solid food. As such, the goal was not high alcohol, at least no higher than necessary to preserve the beer through the fast periods, but instead to carry over as much food value as possible.

This beer did not have a long shelf life. It was prepared for a known, fixed time, and only enough to carry through was made. It was drunk relatively fresh, rather than having a significant lagering period, and had a lower hopping rate. This gave the beer an even sweeter finish, producing a very satiating effect — just the thing required by the monks.

## DUNKLES BOCK

Original Gravity: 1.064-1.072 (16-18 °Plato)
Final Gravity: 1.013-1.019 (3.25-4.7 °Plato)
Apparent Degree of Attenuation: 72-81 percent
Real Degree of Attenuation: 57-65 percent
Alcohol Content: 5-5.8 percent w/v (6.3-7.2 percent v/v)
pH: 4.5-4.7
Bitterness: 20-27 IBUs
Color: 20-30 °SRM (50-78 °EBC)

As a link to the past of Bock beers, this is the standard-bearer of the style from 1614 into this century. Now, however, it has been mostly supplanted by the Helles varieties and finding a commercial example is increasingly difficult. (Curiously, the Hofbräuhaus München, originator of the style, does not currently produce one, but Einbecker Brauhaus, which originally produced a paler beer, does.) Outside of Germany, this is the

Label is from the collection of Charles Finkel.

predominant style, left over from a time when the style emigrated to foreign lands.

The color of a Dunkles Bock is a result of materials and process. The grist used will be of 50 percent or more *dunklesmalz,* or dark malt. In this context, dark malt is what would be commonly termed Munich malt (7 to 8 °SRM/ 14 to 16 °EBC) in the United States. They are called dark malts because they are, naturally enough, darker than pale two-row malt. A small percentage of caramel malt may be added as well (as much as 3 or 4 percent).

The color is increased during a two- or even three-decoction mash, and a long boil. These steps are important to creating an authentic beer. Simple sugars and amino acids combine in a Maillard (or browning) reaction to form melanoidins, which are brown to black pigments. A beer with a high level of melanoidins will have a red-brown to deep-brown color, with garnet highlights.[26] Melanoidins also provide the characteristic malty aroma and flavor of these beers.

This is aided by some slight residual dimethyl sulfide (DMS) character, which adds the "lager" flavor and enhances the malt character. DMS levels, which are detectable at 0.03 mg/L levels and are commonly seen in the 0.08 to 0.10 mg/L range, are still never high enough to become independently recognizable as cooked vegetables, creamed corn, or cabbage. They supply a sulfury undertone that makes these beers crisper and more drinkable than comparable gravity barley wines. The longer boil times associated

**OLD TIME BOCK BEER**

Label is from the collection of Charles Finkel.

with dunkles beers eliminate more of the potential DMS.

The body of a Dunkles Bock is big and bold, yet the beer doesn't have a corresponding powerful sweetness. Some of its sweetness is due to the ethanol content, which also contributes to the full mouth feel of the beer.[27] The high melanoidin content and especially the high percentage of dextrins that result from the grist selection and intensive decoction mashing also add to the rich mouth feel.

Along with these wort production flavors, there are fermentation by-products that affect the flavor and aroma of the beer. The cold temperature fermentations that these beers undergo limit the production of higher alcohols (or *fusel oils*). Most are restricted to levels well below the taste threshold. In analyses of commercial examples,[16,17,28] two exceptions, which may appear at or slightly above the threshold of perception, are isoamyl and phenol alcohols. The former, which can give a solvent or banana character in higher concentrations, can

37

be present in concentrations from one to two times the threshold of 40 mg/L. Phenol alcohols, producing a rose aroma in small concentrations and detectable beginning about 10 mg/L, can appear in concentrations of 12 to 16 mg/L. At these levels, they play the role of secondary flavor constituents and add interesting undertones to the flavor and aroma. They should not be distinctly perceptible.

Similarly, esters should be kept below the sensory threshold. Occasionally, in a commercial beer, one ester or another may actually reach its threshold value. But in such a heartily flavored product, it won't be noticed independently, and can actually add to the "interest" of the beer. As a rule, esters are to be minimized or avoided by strict control of the fermentation. This is an especially critical point as esters almost invariably rise with higher gravity worts. Staying at or below the "interest" (threshold) level for most esters requires strict attention to and control of the fermentation temperature.

Another group of unwanted, potential flavoring components are the vicinal diketones, in particular, diacetyl and 2,3 pentanedione. These compounds can add butter, butterscotch, and honey tones in small quantities (beginning above 0.1 mg/L and 1 mg/L, respectively), and can lead to rancid flavors and aromas in large

Label is from the collection of Charles Finkel.

quantities. Bock beers should not have these flavors. These compounds are formed during the breakdown of pyruvic acid inside the yeast cell, and can leak out into the wort. In a normal fermentation, they will be reabsorbed when the yeast run low on fermentable sugars and then converted to diols which have a very high taste threshold. If the yeast are too flocculant or go dormant before they finish off the sugars in the wort, sometimes fermentation adjustments must be made to avoid leaving these as spillover products. Such adjustments may include inducing a relatively warm period just as the yeast are flocculating out.

Bitterness levels from hops are relatively low. Bitterness obtained from excessive caramelization that might occur either in the boil (from insufficient dilution of extracts or from very hot spots in the kettle) or in a decoction if it is allowed to scorch will add a very unpleasant harshness.

The bitterness plays a background role as a secondary flavor contributor. Typical IBU values range from 17 to 24, not exceeding more than double the threshold value (12 IBU). The bitter character of even the finest noble hops rapidly becomes harsh in the very carbonate water.[29] A high hopping rate would compete with the strong malt flavors and produce a muddy result. Also, a high hopping rate would be exaggerated by the carbonate-induced harshness, and overemphasize the conflict in primary flavors.

Relative to pilseners and other continental beer styles, carbonation levels are low in all the dark Bock styles. Both Dunkles Bock and Doppelbock have carbonation rates generally in the range of 2.1 to 2.3 volumes of $CO_2$ (0.41 to 0.45g $CO_2$/100g beer).

## HELLES BOCK AND MAIBOCK

Original Gravity: 1.064-1.072 (16-18 °Plato)
Final Gravity: 1.012-1.016 (3.0-3.9 °Plato)
Apparent Degree of Attenuation: 76-82 percent
Real Degree of Attenuation: 61-66 percent
Alcohol Content: 5.3-5.9 percent w/v (6.7-7.4 percent v/v)
pH: 4.5-4.7
Bitterness: 23-33 IBUs
Color: 4.6-8 °SRM (9-18 °EBC)

Helles Bock is a relatively recent arrival in the Bock family. Although the original Einbecker beer was described as pale, that is relative to other very dark beers of its day. Helles Bock is the result of scientific investigation and technological advances in malting and brewing. These have produced a beer only half as dark as the palest beer of the past, from resources that had previously enforced the exclusive production of dark beers.

Even so the Helles Bocks are designed to walk a fine line between blandness and too much color. The darker colors that come with large quantities of melanoidins are not wanted, but their flavors and aromas are. To achieve this balance, these beers use dunklesmalz, although the quantities employed are much lower than in a Dunkles Bock beer. From a beer that is one third higher in original gravity than a common pilsener, we see at least two to four times as much color. These beers are in the deep gold to light amber range as a result of this compromise in ingredients.

To make up for the lowered melanoidin flavor and aroma, generally a two-decoction mash is used, with shorter boil times. These shorter boil times result in higher DMS levels that emphasize the "lager" character

Label is from the collection of
Charles Finkel.

and malt aromas. The DMS levels in a Helles Bock can be two to six times the flavor threshold (30 micrograms/L).

Also, more hop bitterness is present than in the Dunkles Bocks to compensate for the missing melanoidins. The water used to make a Helles Bock must be nearly free of carbonates (doing this with waters that are originally strongly imbued with them is one area that required the application of science and technology). This hop bitterness does not take on harsh notes. Instead it is smooth, clean, and refreshing.

Commercial Bock beers tend to have a rather wide range of carbonation: 2.15 to 2.7 volumes of $CO_2$ (0.42 to 0.53g $CO_2$/100g beer). Interestingly, the darker beers tend to be carbonated at the lower end of the scale and the more pale beers at the higher end. But even in those beers that do not follow this general rule, there are few that fall in the range of 2.3 to 2.55 volumes of $CO_2$ (0.45 to 0.50g $CO_2$/100g beer). This "hole" in the carbonation range tends to separate dark from pale beers, but persists even for those that cross over. Generally, Helles Bocks are noticeably more carbonated than the Dunkles Bocks or Doppelbocks.

Maibock is a subtype of the Helles Bocks. It is brewed to the same general specifications as Helles Bock,

Label is from the collection of Charles Finkel.

but with a bit more aging and more hops — up to perhaps 35 IBUs, which would be fairly aggressive in a lower gravity beer. Maibock has a little more color (up to 11 °SRM/25 °EBC) which brings it into the light- to medium-amber range. The hops may even have a cameo appearance in the nose of the beer, but still remain in the background relative to the fresh malty aroma, which is enhanced by the addition of a bit more dark malt. A more assertive version of the Helles Bock, Maibock adds some spice and flair to the reawakening of spring.

### DOPPELBOCK

Original Gravity: 1.072-1.080 (18-20 °Plato)
Final Gravity: 1.016-1.024 (4-6 °Plato)
Apparent Degree of Attenuation: 60-78 percent
Real Degree of Attenuation: 54-62 percent
Alcohol Content: 5.5-6.1 percent w/v (6.9-7.7 percent v/v)

pH: 4.5-4.7
Bitterness: 16-26 IBUs
Color: 20-28 °SRM (52-74 °EBC)

Although technically there is no upper bound on the strength of a Doppelbock, and in fact some extra strong varieties like EKU 28 and Kulmbacher Reichelbräu G'frorns (*frozen*) Eisbock have original gravities well above 1.080 (20 °Plato), almost all "normal" Doppelbocks do appear in this gravity range.

Doppelbocks have a color as dark as, or darker than Dunkles Bocks, and for exactly the same reasons. Their mash makeup, carbonate water, triple decoction mashing process, and long boil times all contribute to the dark brown color with deep red highlights. The increase in original gravity emphasizes the color and the other

Label is from the collection of Charles Finkel.

malt-based characteristics.

Bitterness levels from hops are either maintained at or depressed below the low levels already present in Dunkles Bocks. Because the perceived bitterness from the increased melanoidin content to some extent compensates for the lack of hop bitterness, the reduction in hop bitterness may not be as important.

Most Doppelbocks have a low carbonation rate. There are a few exceptions that can be as high as 2.6 volumes of $CO_2$ (0.51g $CO_2$/100g beer), but these are isolated examples outside the usual range of 2.1 to 2.3 volumes of $CO_2$ (0.41 to 0.45g $CO_2$/100g beer).

Doppelbocks originated independently from Dunkles Bocks, but they have grown closer together over time. The comments on other flavor characteristics mentioned above in the section on Dunkles Bocks apply here equally well.

Especially as Helles Bocks have begun to take over the Bock niche, the darker beers have become crowded together. There are now a few pale Doppelbocks appearing on the market. These pale Doppelbocks are more like Dunkles Bocks than Helles Bocks, with only the color change and lower melanoidin content in flavor and aroma to distinguish them. Without the bitterness as a foil, they are sweeter in taste and finish.

## OTHER BOCK BEER STYLES

**Eisbock:** This is a specialty beer produced by the Kulmbacher Reichelbräu brewery in northern Bavaria. Some craft breweries outside the United States have attempted the style occasionally, but to the author's knowledge, only the Niagara brewery in Canada produces this style regularly. One reason for its rarity may be that extra equipment is needed to produce it. Another, at least within the United States, is that Eisbock production requires a distilling license if the finished beer has an effective gravity higher than its original gravity.

The idea behind Eisbock is that the final product is distilled to some extent by freezing the water and removing the remaining liquid — thereby concentrating all of the flavoring components and the alcohol. By measuring the amount of water removed, the concentration factor can be determined as follows, where $V_{start}$ is the volume of the beer before freezing and $V_{final}$ is the volume of the remaining beer after freezing:

$$\text{Concentration} = \frac{V_{start}}{V_{final}}$$

When the original gravity of the beer is multiplied by this factor, it yields as the result an "effective original gravity." This can then be used to determine the alcohol level of the Eisbock in the usual way.

Because this distillation process concentrates all of the components of the beer, any off-flavors will be concentrated and emphasized. This can make esters particularly noticeable, resulting in very fruity and ale-like flavors. If the original beer had a large concentration of higher alcohols, these will be concentrated and create off-aromas and harsh flavors.

**American Bock:** A difficulty one finds is that the ground which seemed so familiar previously is now beginning to have new entries from many craft breweries. In the United States, Bock beer used to be synonymous with any dark beer. These beers, sometimes brewed to their own recipes and sometimes merely colored versions of their brewery's regular beer, are normally brewed from a standard 1.048 (12 °Plato) wort, and end up with a sweet, caramel taste, but little malt aroma or flavor.

However, new interpretations are appearing on the market from innovative craft brewers. Some have taken the existing American style and used quality flavoring and coloring malts to heighten the malt impact. Others have begun with the style parameters of the classic German styles and given them an American twist by using local ingredients like US two-row malt and Pacific Northwest hop strains.

Finally, some brewers use the name as a jumping-off point for creating altogether new styles, changing one or

Label is from the collection of Charles Finkel.

more of the parameters well out of the existing categories. They produce very hoppy beers, or perhaps beers made with very clean fermenting ale yeasts. These are new products waiting for public reaction.

Label is from the collection of Charles Finkel.

# 3

# Brewing Bock Beer — Materials

It is the raw materials that have shaped Bock beers. The processes that we can analyze to determine where flavors and physical characteristics are formed were devised in order to make better beer from these materials. In the craft environment, one must consider the consequences throughout the brewing process of substitution of materials.[30]

## WATER

As we have seen, the water from Munich has a lot of "temporary" (carbonate) hardness. One analysis of Munich's water lists these ions:

| | | |
|---|---|---|
| Calcium | 75 | mg/L |
| Magnesium | 18 | mg/L |
| Sodium | 2 | mg/L |
| Carbonate | 148 | mg/L |
| Chloride | 2 | mg/L |
| Sulfate | 10 | mg/L |

Without some outside treatment, a pale beer resembling today's Helles Bocks would be impossible to make.

Munich beers were either quite dark or purposely soured until the last century, when the secrets of making pale beers were finally elucidated. At that point, the Munich brewers began to make Helles beer, and eventually, Helles Bock.

In order to brew a dark Bock beer with the relatively dry finish of the traditional Bocks, it is necessary to have a high carbonate content. These carbonates buffer the brewing liquor so that the addition of a large quantity of dark malts won't over-acidify the mash.

It is important to note here the pH of the mash, not the water itself. Water treatment is supposed to affect the brewing water to get the right pH and ion balance in the mash. Measuring the pH of the brewing water can only provide very little information for determining what to do. With soft water, a small amount of basic or acidic material can cause dramatic shifts in pH; this may have already happened and you can't tell this from the pH alone.

Contact your water department and have a water analysis sent to you; this service is free from any public utility or private commercial supplier. If you are on a private well, investigate Noonan's "Water Workshop" article[31] for less expensive ways of discovering the makeup of your water. You can also have a private service test your water for a more complete rundown. Refer to the article in the January 1990 *Consumer Reports* magazine[32] on water testing and purification to learn more about commercially available testing services and different kinds of treatments and their effectiveness and expense.

In many cases, obtaining the necessary levels of carbonates requires the addition or creation of carbonates in the brewing liquor. If this is needed, the water should be soft to begin with, since, besides calcium and carbonate, there is little other ionic content in the Munich water. Adding calcium carbonate ($CaCO_3$) to the water is the natural way to bring up both components at once. Although calcium carbonate is barely soluble in water (19 mg/L),[33] in the acid mash sufficient quantities of calcium carbonate will convert to free calcium and bicarbonate ($HCO_3$).

Another way to add carbonates to water is by utilizing calcium oxide (CaO, lime powder) in a carbonic acid environment:

$$CaO + CO_2 \rightarrow CaCO_3$$

This can be accomplished by adding calcium oxide to water and then chilling and injecting carbon dioxide under pressure or bubbling it through. Supplying an excess of carbon dioxide is not a problem because it will disperse when used in the hot mash. In this way, calcium oxide can be used, part for part, with calcium carbonate.

Other sources of carbonates such as sodium carbonate ($Na_2CO_3$) or sodium bicarbonate ($NaHCO_3$) can also supply much of the needed carbonates, albeit with a substantial contribution of sodium.[34] Potassium equivalents ($K_2CO_3$, $KHCO_3$) may also be used, but potassium tends to have the same flavor effects as sodium. It may be important to try to spread the cation load around by choosing a combination of different salts to achieve the wanted levels of carbonates.

Harder waters may add a salty or metallic character not wanted in this style. Large amounts of sulfate are not appropriate, as this produces an exaggerated drying effect.[35,36] This effect, especially in combination with carbonates, will increase hop bitterness in a harsh manner. It can also cause excessive acidification of the mash. This will reduce the formation of break material in and after the boil, and can lead to haze formation. If your local water contains significantly more than 50 mg/L of sulfate, consider diluting it with distilled water to bring it under this value and then adjusting for both calcium and carbonate concentrations.

For Helles Bocks, the water should be soft, with some calcium. Munich breweries typically treat their water with calcium hydroxide $(Ca(OH)_2)$[36] to precipitate most of the carbonate as $CaCO_3$. Home brewers can boil the water, cooling it quietly, and decant it off of the carbonate precipitate. Another approach is to dilute the carbonate water with distilled water until the combined carbonate content has fallen under 50 mg/L.[36] Soft water is advisable for use in sparging, as well, to keep the pH of the grain bed from rising during lautering.

With most of the carbonate removed, Munich water is much closer to soft, Pilsen type water. Acidification of the mash is not a problem when using the slightly darker Helles malts, or when darkening is increased by decoction mashing, or when some dunkles or caramel malt is added to the grist.

The calcium needed for acidification and yeast health can be added to soft water with some calcium sulfate (gypsum or $CaSO_4$), or with calcium chloride $(CaCl_2)$. Although adding either of these raises the paired ion ($SO_4$, Cl) concentration to levels that wouldn't normally be associated with Munich water, in small amounts their addition won't affect the flavor of the resulting beer. 50 mg/L of calcium is a good level for these purposes.[23]

## MALT

If ever there was a beer style that could be thought

of as varietal, Bock beer would be it. Varietal wines are those wines labeled by grape variety rather than by regional wine making practice such as Chardonnay, compared to a white Bordeaux. As the defining feature of these beers, there should be something special about the malt employed. The favorite selection of German brewers is two-row spring Moravian barley, which is a particularly low protein malt. The Moravian barley strain provides a distinct character which is enhanced in the style.[37] It is grown throughout the countryside of Bavaria and is in widespread planting throughout Europe. All of the malt styles discussed below are typically created from this variety of barley in Europe.

The situation is very different in North America, where high-protein six-row varieties are often used for "specialty" malts such as Munich, caramel, and chocolate.[2,30] Where a continental malt may have 10 percent protein, six-row malt can rarely be found at under 12 percent, and usually the protein level will be closer to 13 percent. In an all-malt beer, especially one like a Bock, there will be sufficient amino acids (called free amino nitrogen, or FAN) for the yeast to do its job, and the additional protein content in a six-row malt can only lead to haze and instability in the final product.

Also, the malting process currently employed in making these North American malts may not necessarily result in the same flavors and aromas as those in European malt. The makeup of North American barley, combined with a shorter, drier, and higher-temperature malting process, results in the product having a different balance of sugars and amino acids and compounds built from them than the European two-row malts. This issue is of prime importance, and is covered in detail below.

Barley seeds are formed from low-moisture starch

granules encased in a tough protein *matrix*. This matrix is what makes the seeds hard and preserves them over winter into the spring. When the embryonic plant senses that spring has arrived, it can manufacture protease, the enzymes needed to dissolve the proteins of the matrix and only then begin to digest the starch.

The term *modification* is commonly interpreted to refer to the level of starch breakdown (and therefore, amylaze enzyme content) in the malt. However, it pertains as much or more to protein degradation as to starch simplification.

Continental European malting practice in the past resulted in malt that was not as friable and soft as American and British malts, which are considered to be adequately- and well-modified, respectively. Continental malts have always been considered to be somewhat under-modified.[36] As recently as 1965, typical Bavarian malt was sprouted only up to the three-quarters point.[38] The embryonic plant was allowed to grow only three quarters of the way around the acrospire. This growth is indicative of the modification level of the malt. British malts are not considered done until the vast majority of seeds show a full length growth of the acrospire.

That has changed, however. Today, imported malts from Germany and Belgium appear to be nearly as modified as their American counterparts. It is entirely possible to use them in single-step infusion mashes, and to expect the same levels of extract as in domestic or British two-row malts.

American two-row strains such as Harrington and Klages provide a different spectrum of proteins, and in greater quantities (typically about 12 percent), which affect the flavors and aromas that arise from the use of these malts.[37] This is, in some respects, done intentionally to enhance the enzyme content of these malts so that high quantities of cereal adjuncts such as corn and rice can be converted. This is an important feature since the largest purchasers of these malts have this purpose in mind when they specify the protein levels needed.

## MELANOIDINS

One of the most important factors in producing quality Bock beers is the creation and maintenance of melanoidins. These colored compounds also provide many of the malty, bready, and beery aromas and flavors that distinguish these styles.

Melanoidins are polymeric compounds formed by nonenzymatic browning, also known as a Maillard reaction,[23] named for the French chemist who elucidated a part of the chemical pathway. The entire process is still not completely understood.

This process occurs when amino acids, the building blocks from which proteins are created, combine instead with simple sugars. In the first step, the amino acid and a sugar molecule combine in an unstable complex that can then either return to the constituent ingredients or be further modified in a reaction known as an Amadori Rearrangement. The result of this is a molecule called a *ketosamine*. Ketosamines gradually break down in acidic, aqueous environments, such as conditions found while mashing or boiling. They can also form complexes, however, with additional sugars (diketosamines), that rapidly decompose under heat into a variety of compounds that are precursors to melanoidins. These precursors, while also being heated, are then converted to melanoidins. Under strong heat (212 degrees F, 100 degrees C), the reaction from ketosamines to melanoidins is definitely favored.

Melanoidins formed from the amino acids glycine and α-alanine give the deepest color while the characteristic malty aromas come from valine and leucine. The former will combine at lower temperatures, the latter only once 212 degrees F or 100 degrees C is reached.[23] Other amino acids form melanoidins as well, but their properties are not yet known. The melanoidins may be responsible for many malty tastes, and the various precursors can, either directly or indirectly, generate the malt aromas that we so love.

Melanoidin production is most active in the malting process, where situations of highly concentrated amino acids and reducing sugars exist. It also continues to some extent in decoction mashing and to a somewhat lesser extent in boiling. For dark beers, it is important to use a malt with a great deal of melanoidins already in it.[37]

The precursors to melanoidins are also subject to modification via a process called Strecker Degradation that produces aldehyde byproducts such as formaldehyde, acetaldehyde, propionaldehyde, isobutyraldehyde, and isovaleraldehyde. These aldehyde compounds are very strong flavoring agents, and it is believed that some of the melanoidin flavors and aromas can be ascribed to them. Many of these aldehydes are carried off in the steam of the boil or further degraded, and the levels carried over into the finished wort are relatively low compared to the initial quantities present in the wort.[39]

However, the aldehydes produced this way are of relatively low molecular weight, and are only somewhat stable. Later, during beer storage, they can undergo transformations into longer-chained aldehydes, which have even lower sensory thresholds and less pleasant flavors and aromas. As the carbon chain in the aldehyde grows beyond six carbon atoms in length, generally the threshold is so low it can be more conveniently expressed in units of $\mu$/L.[22]

Also, one of the principal melanoidin precursors itself is 5-hydroxymethylfurfural, which has been measured at concentrations of up to 78 mg/L in dark beers.[23] This aldehyde and its cousins, furfural and 5-methylfurfural, are also carried over into the finished beer. Fortunately, they have higher taste thresholds (5-hydroxymethylfurfural has a threshold of 1 gm/L and furfural is 150 mg/L), but furfurals are closely associated with stale flavors.

The other danger arising from melanoidins is that they are easily oxidized, especially when they are hot.[40] The oxidation of melanoidins is not a direct problem, but they can later be reduced by alcohols, converting the alcohols into aldehydes, or by polyphenols (tannins) which can then cause haze.[22] Aldehydes, especially those formed from higher (longer carbon chain) alcohols, produce a distinct stale and cardboard flavor.

On the other hand, if melanoidins make it into the beer in a reduced state, they help to maintain the beer by sacrificing themselves first to oxidation, rather than alcohols and polyphenols. As Fix has stated,[22] they are indeed a two-edged sword. The key to producing an extremely stable product is to prevent melanoidin oxidation before packaging, and particularly before cooling of the wort.

Melanoidins are present to a certain extent in all malts, but they can be coaxed into much greater development by careful selection of the barley seed and certain malting techniques. The abundance and balance of amino acids present in the barley and enhanced by the manipulations of the maltster in creating the green malt

(malt ready for kilning) and kilning it, can control which kinds of melanoidin compounds are created.[23] The green malt must be rich in reducing sugars and soluble amino acids to produce an adequate Munich or caramel malt. Since this situation can only be partially controlled by the modification of the seed during steeping and germination, the barley strain is of critical importance. The end result can be an intense malt flavor and aroma, and deep red-brown colors.

## HELLESMALZ (PALE MALT)

2 to 2.7 °Lovibond (2.3 to 4.0 °EBC)

Pale malt will make up the majority of the grain bill for Helles Bocks, and a large fraction of it in the darker colored beers. Especially for the former styles, it is important to use a distinctly flavored malt to produce a memorable and faithful beer.

In a laboratory, this malt can yield 80 to 82 percent of its dry weight up for conversion into sugars and dextrins, and soluble proteins. In a brewery situation, somewhat less yield can be expected.

Typically, this malt will go through a drying phase and very light kilning to produce a relatively pale colored malt that still has some melanoidin character. After the germination process produces the correct level of modification in the green malt, it will undergo a twelve-hour drying phase followed by four hours of kilning. Generally, the drying temperature will be 122 degrees F (50 degrees C), and kilning will occur at 176 degrees F (80 degrees C).[41]

The drying phase makes use of the enzymes that have been created during germination to solibulize and break down a lot of the protein matrix. This comes from the action of peptidases, glucanases, and phosphatases. The resulting malt is therefore soft, and this allows the starch granules to be easily liberated during the mash. Some amount of simple sugars are also created, even at this low temperature. The drying phase brings the green malt from about 40 percent water down to about 10 percent.

The kilning process finishes drying the malt, taking the water content down to between 3.5 and 4 percent, which allows the malt to have a long storage life. The low water content tends to help preserve the various enzyme systems in the malt so that they will be available when the malt is mashed.

Helles malt is the only kind of malt that can have any β-glucanase surviving into the finished malt; the higher temperatures used in making other malts completely destroys this fragile enzyme. The β-glucanase enzyme moderates the breakdown of β-glucans, which increase viscosity and slow down lautering.

Kilning also helps to add some coloring and malty aroma by creating a small amount of melanoidins from some simple sugars and liberated amino acids. The low temperature processing determines that only a few of these compounds, particularly the lighter colored and flavored ones, are produced.[23]

In the end, helles malt is a very specialized product that is a compromise between light color and rich flavor. This compromise is especially suited to the production of all Munich styled beers, and in particular, Helles Bocks.

## DUNKLESMALZ (MUNICH MALT)

5 to 9 °Lovibond (9.5 to 21 °EBC)
True Munich malt is a very specialized product. The

approach of darkening malt by heating it after it is dry does not imitate the character of the real thing.[37] The key to making Munich malt is to use relatively high temperatures while the green malt is still wet to enhance melanoidin production. In this sense, Munich malt is more closely related to caramel malt than to pale malt, although it does retain sufficient enzyme activity to convert its starch content to sugars.

Several steps are taken to insure increased melanoidin levels. More total enzymes are created, and more amino acids and simple sugars are liberated by first "forcing" the piece of malt (as maltsters phrase it) to a high level of modification during germination.[37] This intensive modification lowers the total extract available to the brewer, but increases the amount of amino acids and reducing sugars present as the green malt is removed to the kiln. Even so, dunklesmalz will yield 77 to 80 percent in the laboratory.

During the drying phase, the green malt is heated to 149 to 158 degrees F (65 to 70 degrees C), where more sugars are created from the starch. Then, the malt is slowly dried at increased temperatures of about 212 to 220 degrees F (100 to 105 degrees C).[41] At these temperatures and with reducing sugars and amino acids present in high concentrations, the melanoidin formation process (as described above) is greatly enhanced. Once 195 degrees F (90 degrees C) is reached, the process really takes off. At temperatures above 212 degrees F (100 degrees C), the color can triple or quadruple the result of drying at 175 degrees F (80 degrees C). The sugars used to create the melanoidins comprise only 2 to 3 percent of the weight of the dried malt, so extract levels are not greatly affected by the melanoidin forming process.

In addition to increased color and aroma formation

from this regimen, other protein removal processes are at work as well. The high temperature enhances protein coagulation and nonenzymatic protein destruction. As a result, Munich malt has a much lower content of high molecular weight proteins, and is much less inclined to form protein hazes in dark beers. Especially during decoction mashing, a tremendous amount of protein is coagulated and removed from the wort before it ever gets into the kettle.

## CARAMELMALZ
## (CARAMEL OR CRYSTAL MALT)

Although this style of malt is originally of English invention, the Germans have adapted it into their own version. Caramel malt is used as a small adjunct, with a maximum of 3 to 5 percent of the grist for pale beers and as much as 10 percent for dark beers. In a pale beer, a lower color malt will be used (20 to 28 °Lovibond / 50 to 70 °EBC), while darker beers may use a combination of pale and dark caramel (40 to 47 °Lovibond / 100 to 120 °EBC) malts. Caramel malt is used to increase malt character, color, and aid head retention.[41] By choosing the caramel malt color carefully, the amount of darkening can be controlled for pale beers.

Caramel malts are created by stewing: the green malt is brought up to 40 to 45 percent water by weight and held between 140 and 167 degrees F (60 to 75 degrees C) for up to three hours. This allows both the protease and amylaze enzymes in the malt to do their work, creating a wealth of simple amino acids and sugars. Then the malt is dried at 300 to 355 degrees F (150 to 180 degrees C) for one to two hours, which builds a high content of melanoidins. The darker the malt, the less extract remains after this color formation. Caramel malts will produce from 70 to 77 percent yield, depending on the original barley and the final color.

## FARBESMALZ (ROASTED MALT)

It may seem curious that the malt that is commonly called Munich malt in North America is known to the Germans as dark malt, while roasted malts like black patent and chocolate are called color malts. This has more to do with how the malt is put to use, rather than with the actual characteristics of the malt itself. Dark malt is used to make dark(er) beers, while color malt is used strictly as a coloring agent.[39]

Color malts should never be used in quantities large enough to significantly affect the flavor or aroma of the beer. Typically, color malts make up at most 1 to 2 percent of the grist.[38] This is because they are roasted to such high temperatures that the malt character they would have had from the melanoidins is overcome by the bitter flavors of burnt caramel and proteins.

At the end of the process, the color malt has a water content of only 1 to 2 percent. Normally, this would increase the percentage of the other components of the malt, but even with this, the malt can produce only about 70 percent extract.

Note also that roasted barley, a common ingredient in Irish and British style beers and widely used in North America, is never used in Germany. This is due to the Reinheitsgebot's prohibition of unmalted cereal ingredients. This prohibition includes unmalted barley.

# MALT SYRUPS AND DRIED MALT EXTRACTS

Malt syrups and dried malt extracts offer the great convenience of achieving the high original gravities needed for these styles without a long, complex process. This is because they can be diluted to just the right level. However, they have their own difficulties, and I am unaware of any commercial German brewer using these ingredients to produce Bock beers.

The problems with extracts are three: potential oxidation in handling and storage, low FAN content, and adulteration with sugar syrups. These problems can be avoided and excellent beer can be created with extracts, but doing so requires getting fresh product from a reliable source, and performing a mini-mash to help overcome problems that might arise from the latter two areas.

It is critical to the quality of the beer, and of dark beer specifically, that it be created with unoxidized wort.[40] As has been made clear in the professional and homebrewing literature, the melanoidins which are so crucial to the flavor and stability of Bock beers will quickly cause the beer to become stale and unpalatable once oxidized.[22] Oxidized melanoidins are at the beginning of several different oxidation reaction chains (mentioned above in the section on melanoidins) that can cause problems with haze and off-flavors. Any oxygen that might be included in the malt extract during the packaging process will have a long period before connecting with the melanoidins in the wort.

Oxidation also increases wort color. An increase of oxygen content from 0.2 mg/L to 1.0 mg/L can increase wort color by 0.38 °SRM (1 °EBC). A further increase to 10.0 mg/L can add another 1.4 °SRM (3.5 °EBC). This darkening does not come with the same aromas and flavors expected from good quality malts.

Darkening can be increased during extended storage times due to the Maillard reactions continuing unabated. In these conditions, a high concentration of reducing sugars and free amino acids are present. However, the different (lower) storage temperatures emphasize formation of a different balance of melanoidins than are created in the high temperature malting, mashing, and boiling processes.[37] This is why it is important to get fresh extract.

Long storage times are sometimes encountered with the distribution and retailing of malt extracts. Ask your supplier when they received their shipment; encourage them to find out how long their distributor has had it. If you start with old extract, your beer could be old even before it has finished lagering.

Other concerns, that have been reported in many publications,[42,43,44,45] indicate that nearly all of forty-four commercial lager extracts purchased from maltsters and from home brewing retailers in Canada had significantly lowered levels of free amino nitrogen (FAN). Many levels had lowered below the point where proper yeast metabolism could be maintained in a standard beer wort of 1.048 (12 °Plato). Some of these extracts had levels that were only half or a third of the generally recommended minimum of 150 mg/L. A Bock beer wort created exclusively from one of these extracts, in spite of the higher original gravity (and correspondingly higher FAN concentration), could still fall at or below the minimum FAN requirements. Further evidence[42,45] shows that FAN utilization by yeast in an extract wort is significantly reduced, regardless of the initial FAN concentration. This evidence leads to the concern that the FAN present has undergone some change during processing that renders it less available to the yeast.

It is not clear why this comes about. One might speculate that as the extract ages and the Maillard reactions continue, a significant fraction of the FAN becomes bound up in melanoidins. If this were to prove true, fresh extract would again be the appropriate solution, but the experiment has not been conducted. Regardless, reduced FAN levels can be counteracted by adding fresh malt back into the beer wort by doing a mini-mash.

Another consideration in examining the use of extracts was reported in the *Journal of the American Society of Brewing Chemists*.[42] Disturbingly enough it was reported that significant evidence of apparent adulteration of some extracts with glucose syrups had been found. (Unfortunately it is unclear who is at fault for the detected adulteration, thus concrete action has yet to be taken.) This not only has the effect of diluting what FAN is available but changes the sugar balance of the resulting wort. This change can have a profound effect on the yeast, because yeast uptake of sugars follows a fixed schedule. Since yeast metabolizes sugars in a rigid order, with single chain sugars used first, high quantities of them suppress the uptake of more complex sugars like maltose.

In a normal all-malt Bock wort, glucose makes up about 25 percent of the carbohydrates; maltose and maltotriose make up as much as 45 percent[38] (dextrins and other minor sugars make up the rest). A wort created from an adulterated extract could easily have these percentages reversed. In such a situation, the Crabtree effect can inhibit the yeast from entering the respiration phase,[22] thus preventing the high reproduction rates needed early in the fermentation to obtain the optimal yeast density in the beer. This can lead to long, disordered fermentations, which can provide opportunities for invading organisms to gain a beachhead in the wort. Indeed, *Journal of the American Society of Brewing Chemists*[42] notes that comparisons of attenuation of the original 1.048 (12 °Plato) wort were cut off after reaching 1.024 (6 °Plato), rather than the planned 1.012 (3 °Plato), because some of the test worts created from extracts never reached their appropriate final gravities.

Dried malt extract (DME) is created by spraying hot wort through a partial vacuum (which lowers the boiling point of the water in the wort), evaporating the water and leaving the wort solids behind. One of the conveniences of DME is that it is easy to measure out and divide up.

However, once the package is opened, another factor comes into play. DME is very hygroscopic, meaning that it will pull moisture out of the air, and begin to liquefy. It is the liquefaction that allows oxidation reactions to proceed, so this must be prevented. DME, once opened, should be kept in a closed, cool, dry environment. A refrigerator or freezer is a good location, since the cold air can hold much less moisture.

There is no information regarding possible adulteration of DME[42,45] as only extract syrups were tested.

Another point of consideration in choosing an extract product: one should be guided by the intended use described on the extract's label. Extracts made from lager malts should provide more of the sulfury, lager character that will help to distinguish the flavor and aroma characteristics of these beers. Extracts made from continental malts have a better chance of containing the crucial melanoidin balance that is wanted.

The greatest difficulty in recommending extracts is

that the evidence shows they can be quite variable from brand to brand.[42]

One should attempt to get the freshest product, from a well known and respected source. Store it in a cool place once purchased, and use it up quickly. Once an extract is discovered that produces a quick and complete fermentation, patronize the producer. Extracts are not interchangeable parts of a beer, and a bargain price does not always purchase a quality product.

The bottom line on extracts is that they can make the process far shorter and more convenient, but insufficient information is available to guide the brewer in making the correct product choice. By formulating recipes with significant amounts of added malts in a mini-mash, potential problems can usually be minimized. This is particularly important for Bock beers, that depend so heavily on the quality of the malt aroma and flavor.

## HOPS

Because bitterness can be discussed easily in terms of quantifiable levels, this tends to overshadow other considerations when choosing boiling hop varieties. Realize that even though such hops are usually discussed only in terms of the bitterness they bring to the beer, they will also contribute differing flavors. Bitterness is only one dimension of hop character, even in hops boiled an hour or more.

Hopping rates are affected by the kind of brewing liquor in use. If the brewing liquor is highly carbonate, as is the case with traditional Dunkles and Doppelbocks, smaller quantities of noble hops should be used in order to maintain the elegance of the beer. Carbonates enhance the perception of bitterness from the hops.[36] Carbonate waters have been called "hop savers",[29] but in fact, they emphasize the strong bitterness of the hops and tend to hide the finer flavors. High $\alpha$-acid hops are particularly affected by this, and yield very rough, coarse flavors that quickly become unpleasant.

Physical characteristics can be important as well. Even though the higher gravity wort of a Bock beer will tend to reduce the amount of bitterness available from the hops,[46] the decreased bittering rates keep the total mass of hops used low. Because hops help to coagulate proteins and therefore clarify the beer, the tiny quantities of high $\alpha$-acid hops that might be called for on the basis of bitterness alone could prove insufficient for clarification purposes. This is especially so in a high protein wort such as a Bock. This could be further emphasized by other processing choices like a shorter boiling time and an infusion, rather than decoction mash.

The most local product for Bavaria comes from the Hallertauer region south and east of Nürnberg. Hersbrucker or Hallertauer Mittelfrüh are the most highly prized products of the Hallertauer region.

In Helles Bocks, where carbonate levels will be low, higher hopping rates should be used, but the fine noble flavors of Hersbrucker, Hallertauer Mittelfrüh, Spalter, and even Tettnanger are still preferred. These give the cleanest, most elegant, and balanced flavors to the beer.

American varieties of the Hallertauer strain, like Mount Hood and Liberty, also work well in Bock beers because they have similar flavor and aroma characteristics to their German forebears.

Other, more distinctive, varieties can be used in blends to tame them a bit. Saaz, Styrian Goldings, and some English and English-derived strains like Kent

Goldings, Fuggles and Willamette can be used in blends with the more traditional hops mentioned above to give unique flavor and aroma notes. Although these would produce less traditional beers, they would not be so strange as to break the Bock beer mold.

The strongly floral and very distinctive citrus flavor of Cascades can fight with the malt and lager characters of Bock beers. Although the author doesn't find this an appealing combination, especially in Helles Bocks, with North American brewers looking for very distinctive products, this elicits partisans on both sides.

## YEAST

The yeast pitched must be a good strain in excellent condition, for the rigors of a high-gravity wort fermentation can otherwise prevent the completion of the task. There must be a large quantity of yeast, and it must already be acclimated. Only when the yeast is at its peak, can it produce a clean product that is free of off-flavors.

The high original gravity, combined with the high final ethanol content work together to inhibit yeast activity. The high concentration of sugars creates osmotic pressure on the yeast cell which, without effort on the part of the cell, would draw water out of the cell's cytoplasm. This effort distracts the cell from other metabolic endeavors, like reproduction, respiration, and fermentation.

Ethanol, as a waste product, is toxic to yeast. This effect is heightened as the fermentation progresses and ethanol concentration goes up. In some cases,[47] this can cause the complete cessation of fermentation well short of the attenuation limit of the wort. Worts with starting gravities above 1.096 (24 °Plato) never reach the attenuation limit with lager yeast.

The strain of yeast chosen should be a known performer, capable of working in a high-gravity environment and still completing the fermentation. It should produce as neutral a flavor as possible, since fermentative byproducts are generally perceived as flaws in the Bock styles.

It must not be of a highly flocculative nature; such yeast strains do not stay in suspension long enough to complete the fermentation, and so the resulting beer will be sickly sweet. In such a situation, the yeast may also leave a strong, unwanted diacetyl component. This

A portion of Emil Hansen's original pure culture yeast propogation equipment, at the Carlsberg brewery in Copenhagen, Denmark. The various inlets and outlets allow the device to be cleaned, filled with wort, have the beer removed, and have the yeast obtained without ever having to open it. Photo by Darryl Richman.

comes about because the yeast falls out of solution before all the sugars are used up, forcing it to metabolize the diacetyl produced early in the fermentation.

Yeast propagation is discussed further in the recipe chapter, but it must be kept in mind that yeast grown on a medium without maltose will require an adaptation period of as much as a day, slowing the start of the fermentation.[47] Although optimum yeast reproduction can be obtained with continually replenished and aerated weak (0.5 percent) sugar solutions, such yeasts are not adapted to brewery conditions. Typically, yeast propagation in the brewery is accomplished with all-malt wort.

The author has had good results with both commercially available strains and those collected from continental and large breweries in the United States. Any strain with good alcohol tolerance that meets the other requirements set forth already will produce a fine Bock. Wyeast Bavarian (2206) is a good place to start. Mixed reports have been aired on Wyeast Munich (2308). Apparently it is somewhat unstable and can produce high levels of diacetyl, therefore requiring special handling (a diacetyl rest) at the end of the primary. Wyeast Bohemian (2124) tends to produce more esters than are called for in the style.

If the brewer is interested in attempting the reproduction of beers from previous centuries, there is room for greater creativity. Before the middle 1800s, single cell cultures were unknown, and mixed cultures of ale yeast were the rule. Lagering has always been practiced to some extent, though, with regard to these styles, so an ale strain that is cold-tolerant is important. Alt beer strains, such as Wyeast German Ale (1336) come to mind, but the ever popular Sierra Nevada/Narragansett yeast (Wyeast American 1056) seems to be tolerant of temperatures down to 50 degrees F (10 degrees C). Both of these strains are good fermenters and do not produce high levels of esters or diacetyl.

The further back in history one goes, the more likely it becomes that some level of lactic acid producers would have been included in the microflora. One should turn to the practices of the rural Belgian brewers for a view back in time. (Suggested reading is *Lambic* by Jean Xavier Guinard.)[24]

# 4

# Brewing Bock Beer — Equipment and Procedures

Most of the techniques employed in brewing Bock beers are the same as those used in brewing other German lager beers. A four-vessel system is employed to perform a two- or three-decoction mash, which is lautered; the wort obtained is then boiled. The boiling may go on for a longer than normal period to increase wort concentration. Cooling is performed quickly and then a pure strain of lager yeast, as previously discussed, is pitched in relatively high quantities. The primary fermentation is conducted at 41 to 48 degrees F (5 to 9 degrees C) for one to two weeks (more likely the latter). Then a long period of lagering at 32 to 34 degrees F (0 to 1 degrees C) is employed to finish the beer. Lagering may continue for two to six months, depending on the brewer and the beer.

## BREWING EQUIPMENT

Standard practice in making Bock beers, as with most of the German lager styles, is the two- or three-decoction mash. The former is employed for Helles

Bocks and a few Dunkles and Doppelbocks, while the latter is used exclusively for the darker varieties. A decoction mash continues the melanoidin building process, aids in protein breakdown and coagulation, and maximizes the gelatinization of the starches in the malt.

The standard four-vessel brewing system is composed of a mash tun, a mash cooker, a lauter tun, and a kettle. Mashing proceeds by doughing-in into the mash tun, and then pumping a portion of the mash off to the cooker, where it will go through a step program of rises and eventually be boiled. This will then be returned to the mash tun, causing the whole mash to raise to the next rest.

This process is repeated once or twice to effect the brewmaster's mash step program. Once mashing is complete, the mash is pumped out of the mash tun into the lauter tun. From there, the wort is strained out and its volume increased by sparging. The clear liquid obtained is transferred to the kettle, where it is boiled and hopped.

Variations on this arrangement are common. The four-vessel system can be easily adapted to three- and even two-vessel arrangements. There is no technical reason to have a separate lauter tun from the mash tun. However, this means that the tun is in use while lautering proceeds, preventing a second mash from starting. The limitation on overlapping brew sessions lowers the overall throughput on the equipment.

A two-vessel system would include the changes needed for the three-vessel system, and further combine the function of the mash cooker with the kettle. Again, this reduces the amount of overlap that is possible between two successive batches, because the second mash cannot begin until the boil of the first batch is

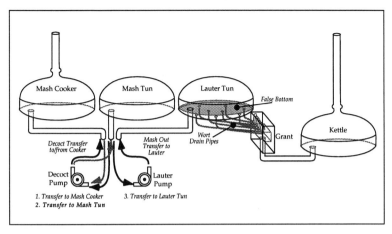

Four vessel system

finished.

For the home brewer, considerations of staggered brewing schedules are fairly low on the priority list. Curiously, decoction mashing requires less equipment than step infusion mashing, and the same as single infusion mashing. A brewing pot and a lauter tun are the requirements for decoction mashing.

## MASHING

The goals of the mashing program for a Bock beer are to produce a high extract wort with a lot of malt character. Low molecular weight proteins and longer chain sugars are emphasized. Little in the way of unconverted starch or polyphenolic material (tannins) should make its way out of the mash.

Traditional mashing programs can be comprised of two decoctions or three; the decoctions can be quick or intensive; and they can include two, three, four, or even five different rest temperatures. Such a wide variety of parameters allows fine control of the finished product, but also makes for a confusing array of choices.

The choice of the number of decoctions and the duration of the boil provides control over the amount of darkening that occurs, protein coagulation, and malt sugar composition.

The decoction process begins when a portion of the mash, the decoct (or thick mash — the portion with the most solids), is brought into the mash cooker. It goes through a step mashing program, just as a step infusion mash would, with the exception that after the last saccharification step, the thick mash is then raised to boiling and held there for an extended period.

The decoct's step program uses whatever enzymes are carried over into the cooker to convert the heavy proteins and starches that are brought along in the malt solids. The final boiling explodes any balled starch that may not have been affected by the chemical action. It also removes longer chained proteins in two ways; by degrading the protein structure through the mechanical action of the boil and the heat breakdown, and by complexing with polyphenols (the same action that is seen again in the kettle boil, when hop polyphenols can combine with malt proteins). This material will then have another opportunity for breakdown into FAN and sugars in the second and, if conducted, third decoction.

Once the decoction has boiled, it is pumped back into the mash tun, where it is mixed with the remaining thin rest mash. The addition of the heat energy brought by the boiling decoct raises the whole mash to the next temperature rest. The mash is allowed to rest for a few minutes before the next thick mash is removed again to the mash cooker. The thin mash remaining behind continues to rest until the next decoction is complete.

A typical grist bill for a dark Bock beer might be 86.3 percent Munich malt, 10 percent helles malt, 2.5 percent caramel malt, and 1.2 percent black malt.[38] This combination would produce a wort color of 9 °Lovibond (20 °EBC). A pale Bock could have half helles malt, half Munich malt, and perhaps a small amount of pale caramel malt. The black malt would be omitted altogether.

The ratio of mash water to malt should be approximately 1.4 quarts per pound (3 L/kg).[39] Although this may seem to be a looser mash than in conventional mashing, the extended mash period and lengthy decoction boils will remove a significant amount of mash liquor as steam. The extra liquid also helps to differentiate the thickest portion of the mash from the thinner, tending to retain more of the mash enzymes in the solution. The mash liquor can therefore act as a reservoir from which enzymes can be drawn as needed, preserving them from boiling.

Doughing-in is accomplished in a chamber that connects the incoming crushed malt line with a mashing vessel. This chamber has a water line also, and, depending on whether the dough-in water is cold or already heated, the vessel is either the mash cooker or the mash tun, respectively.

The arrangement of the chamber and the water injection creates a great deal of turbulence. This effectively mixes the grist and limits the amount of starch that balls up. Especially for decoction mashing, it is important to get all of the malt flour into solution. This liberates the various proteolytic and diastatic enzymes, ensuring that most of them will be maintained safely in the thin mash where they can do their jobs, rather than going into the mash cooker with the thick mash where they will be degraded.

Once dough-in is accomplished, if the dough-in water was cold, the entire mash is heated in the mash cooker to about 100 degrees F (37 degrees C). Otherwise, the temperature of the mash water is chosen to produce a mash at this temperature. The temperature necessary is dependent on the water to malt ratio, but generally a temperature of about 110 degrees F (43 degrees C) will work.

The first thick mash is separated from the rest mash. This thick mash should have a liquor to malt ratio of 1 quart per pound (2.2 L/kg). For the craft-brewer, this can only be estimated. Pulling the decoct from the bottom of the tun, after allowing the total mash to rest for five minutes, will select the right mix.

If the dough-in occurred in the mash cooker, the rest mash is pumped to the mash tun. Otherwise, the thick mash is pumped to the mash cooker.

The common wisdom, that a thick mash of a third of the total mash volume will be sufficient to raise the entire mash to the next rest, rarely proves to be true. There are many variables that come into play, including the insulating qualities of the mash tun, the surface area-to-volume ratio of the mash as it sits in the tun, and exactly how "thick" the thick mash is (e.g., where the thick mash is extracted from, how long the mash rests before the thick mash is extracted, and so forth).

Experience with the equipment is the best teacher. Unfortunately, it is not likely that a pilot brew will be helpful, as a pilot brewery will not have the same thermal properties as the full scale brewhouse. The best hedge is to estimate high on the thick mash volume and adjust downwards as experience is gained. A good starting point might be about 40 percent of the total mash volume. It should go without saying that scrupulous records need to be kept in the early stages of working out the decoction mash schedule with any particular equipment system.

During each of the decoctions, the mash must be stirred continuously as it is heated to prevent sticking, scorching, and burning. These flavors can easily be detected in the final product, and they are not a pleasant addition. Care must be taken that the mash cooker is appropriately sized and heated. If too little mash is placed in a very hot cooker, it will easily burn. On the other hand, the stirring must be done carefully so as not to splash, which could encourage significant hot side aeration.[40] This can result in the oxidation of both melanoidins and, particularly at the high end of the saccharification range around 154 to 162 degrees F (68 to 72 degrees C), polyphenols.[39]

If working by hand, this can be accomplished by holding the mash paddle at a point slightly above the surface of the decoct with the weaker hand and using the stronger hand to turn the top of the mash paddle in an elliptical pattern. This breaks the surface the least, introducing the smallest amount of air. Heavy rubber gloves are advised since some splashing may still occur, especially when the worker grows tired.

The diagram that follows shows a mash program used at the Bavarian State Brewery at Weihenstephan. It is typical of a full blown, three-decoction mash. That the mash process takes a full six and a half hours is not an error.

Each decoct goes through a full step mash program in order to ensure that the malt is as fully utilized as possible. In this case, the three-decoction mash program has mash cooker rests at 127 degrees, 149 degrees, and 162

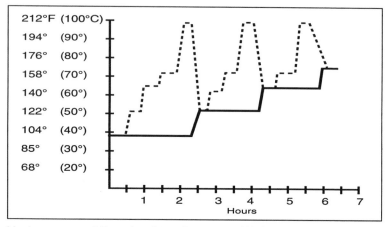

Mash program at Bavarian State Brewery at Weihen – Stephan: Typical three-decoction mash program.

degrees F (53 degrees, 65 degrees, and 72 degrees C) before going on to boiling.

Recent work[48] shows that the protein rest is only effective in extended (30 minutes or longer), concentrated mashes, such as those that occur in the rest mash and especially in the decoct. The protein rest is responsible for generally reducing the overall length of all protein molecules in the mash. In so doing, it tends to eliminate the longest proteins, which could otherwise cause foam instability (by reducing the surface tension in the beer) and haze (by complexing with polyphenols). It also liberates a large quantity of FAN by breaking it free from the longer chained protein molecules, which is critical to yeast growth.

The saccharification rests in the decoct are interesting; they occur at the extreme low and high ends of the range, 149 to 160 degrees F (65 to 72 degrees C). The goal in doing this, as opposed to employing a single rest in the middle of the range, is to emphasize the production of dextrins. A single rest in the middle of the saccharification range would cause both α- and β-amylaze enzymes to be active at close to their maximal levels, allowing the β-amylaze to further degrade linear branches of starch and dextrin chopped free by the α-amylaze. A separate low rest allows the β-amylaze enzymes to do only as much work as is possible with the available linear chains of sugars; the following high temperature rest then allows the α-amylaze enzymes to degrade the branched starch molecules into dextrins.

High dextrin content helps to create the rich character expected in the beer style. In particular, lower molecular weight dextrins (less than 12 glucose molecules long) increase head retention and help to provide a finer carbonation. Dark beers are generally distinguished from pale beers by the lower content of maltose and the higher content of dextrins.[38] Dark beers are more likely to go through an extended triple decoction mash like this.

The decoct should show a negative reaction to iodine at the completion of the last step, 160 degrees F (72 degrees C), before proceeding on to boiling. This final step inactivates all of the enzymes present in the decoct. Full use should be made of them before they are lost.

The second decoction should likewise be a thick mash, and should proceed through the remaining temperature steps before going to a boil. The third decoction can be either another thick mash,[38] or a thinner mash (sometimes called a lauter mash) of 40 percent of the total mash volume.[39] In the latter case, the intention is to assure more fully the destruction of any remaining diastatic enzymes, in order to preserve the sugar and dextrin makeup of the wort.

Meanwhile the rest mash temperature plateaus should be reached at 100 degrees, 127 degrees, 149 degrees, and 167 degrees F (37 degrees, 53 degrees, 65 degrees, and 75 degrees C). The first rest is achieved at dough-in with warm water. The others are attained with the reintroduction of each successive decoct. The sum of the times spent by the decoct at each mash cooker rest determine the total time the rest mash spends at each of its temperature rests.

The second rest at 127 degrees F (53 degrees C) is used to degrade proteins and to enhance foam stability and β-glucans. High quality malt is a necessary ingredient, as it will have the lowest levels of β-glucans to start with. These compounds increase wort viscosity and can dramatically increase lautering times and sparging volumes. Longer and more intensive mashing breaks down more of the β-glucans and can reduce viscosity by as much as a third.[40] High-quality pale malt will have retained some β-glucanase, an enzyme that degrades β-glucans, even after malting. This enzyme is active below 140 degrees F (60 degrees C), but will be destroyed at higher temperatures.

The emphasis on dextrin production continues in the rest mash process. Looking at the temperatures shows that once again there is no rest in the middle of the saccharification range. Instead, a rest at the low end of the range, 149 degrees F (65 degrees C) is followed by a final rest at the high end of the range, 167 degrees F (75 degrees C). This last rest is for mash off. A negative iodine reaction should have been achieved in the rest mash before the final decoct is returned to the mash tun.

A two-decoction mash is becoming more common for dark Bocks as a means of conserving energy and reducing the amount of time required in the brewhouse. However, it is still the exception and not the rule; more often the two-decoction mash is only employed in pro-

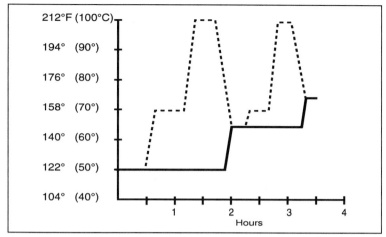

Typical two-decoction mash program.

ducing Helles Bocks.

The reason for this is that the balance of flavors produced in a two-decoction mash is different from the longer and more intensive three-decoction mash. With less concentration of the mash, darkening due to melanoidin formation and caramelization is reduced. Other flavors in the beer arising from the remaining ingredients can, as a result, come to the fore.

A typical two-decoction mash program is diagrammed above. Here the acidification rest is dropped and with it, a very long decoction cycle is eliminated, cutting the mashing time to three and one-half hours.

The temperature rests are slightly different as well: the rest mash goes through a low saccharification rest at 149 degrees F (65 degrees C), and a mash off at 167 degrees F (75 degrees C). The decocts, instead, have a single rest at 158 degrees F (70 degrees C), which is at the high end of the saccharification rest. This combination is intended to produce a high dextrin content in the resulting wort, in spite of the compromise in the process. Even so, the difference between a pale and a dark Bock beer wort is that the dark wort will have a lower concentration of maltose and a higher level of dextrins and melanoidins.

## INFUSION MASHING

Infusion mashing, especially for Bock beers, is nearly unheard of in Bavaria. The brewers interviewed for this book claimed that infusion mashing did not allow enough malt character to be extracted from the malt, did not provide as much extract, produced more starch and higher proteins, and yielded less color. It also does not allow for the sharp temperature changes that provide finer control over the balance of sugars produced during the mash.

These complaints are all true, but North American brewmasters, with an investment in an infusion system, can still make beers in the classic style. Other parameters will just have to be adjusted to make up for the problems.

The recipes in the next chapter are based on numbers that the author obtains on his equipment. Brewers must look at their own equipment, though, and adjust material quantities based on their circumstances. Extract levels should be calculated based on each brewer's own experience.

Melanoidins are at the heart of most of the aromas and the color that is needed for beers of this style. (Lack of DMS character may only be a problem with two-row ale malts.)[49] From the melanoidin discussion in the previous chapter, it can be realized that an infusion mash never gets hot enough for long enough to really drive the Maillard process. It cannot cause significant amounts of reducing sugars to combine with amino acids and proceed through the sequence of reactions that produce melanoidins. The two or three decoctions, which can call for boiling the thick, concentrated mash for as much as an hour, can cause significant darkening, indicating melanoidin formation is proceeding.

By working with increased quantities of caramel malts, and also including a long boil, more melanoidins can be included or formed. In the author's experience, a wort created from a grain bill of 60 to 80 percent Munich malt and up to 10 percent of 20 to 40 °Lovibond (50 to 100 °EBC) caramel malt will produce a first wort that is pumpkin orange. (Do not attempt to make up for the lack of color by using substantial quantities of black malt. Remember that the Germans call these *color* malts because they are used for their coloring properties only. The heavy presence of roasted, coffee or ashy flavors that these malts can impart is not appropriate for the traditional style beer.) Combining a thorough (but not too thorough — see the section on lautering, just ahead) sparging to collect perhaps an extra third to half of the final volume, and then subjecting that to a very long boil of two and a half or three hours, will reduce the volume and increase the color into the 20 to 30 °Lovibond (50 to 65 °EBC) range of deep browns.

The remaining complaints regarding infusion mashing, that more starch and higher proteins are extracted than from a decoction mash, result directly from the less intensive processing. These problems can be cured by a long, very cold, lagering period. This will allow some polyphenols to gradually combine with higher weight proteins and drop out of solution. Starches will also tend to fall out of solution over time. A brewer might consider finings if a brilliantly clear beer could not be achieved.

(The author has not needed them in the past to produce clear beers.)

So, some of the resistance to infusion mashing may be hide-bound tradition, some of it may be the cost of materials, and a part may be prejudice reflecting a "not-invented-here" point of view. Energy costs and process time are a place where infusion mashing certainly comes out ahead; the savings are obtained by eliminating the long heating times needed for each decoction step.

However, there is still room for the consideration that decoction does produce a more flavorful and aromatic product. It is a distinctly different technique, producing a different result in the end, not just a more involved way of achieving particular rest temperatures.

## LAUTERING

At the end of the mashing process, the entire mash is brought into the lauter tun and allowed to settle for perhaps ten minutes. At this point, a substantial amount of the original volume will have been reduced. (An example shows an original mash liquor volume of 61 hL reduced to 40 hL when the mash reached the lauter tun following a six and one-half hour triple decoction.)[38]

The wort contained in the mash will be of a higher specific gravity than the intended original gravity for the beer. This is necessary because the wort will be diluted during sparging. In the example cited above, the gravity is almost 28 percent over the original gravity of the beer itself.

Recirculation is begun and continues until the wort runs clear. There are competing reasons for shorter and longer recirculation periods. A long recirculation, which minimizes the carry over of malt solids and precipitated proteins into the boiling kettle, also tends to strip out wort lipids freed during the mash. These lipids are important to yeast cell wall creation, and even though the continental two-row malts tend to be significantly higher in lipids than North American or British malts, the stripping action can still be overdone.

Shorter recirculation periods will tend to carry over more solids. This is believed to be an advantage by some, who feel that the solids provide nucleation sites for the agglomeration of proteins during the boil, thus producing clearer worts at the end of the boil. On the other hand, the haze that may be brought into the boil along with the solids carries higher weight proteins. These can cause chill haze in the final product. In a richer beer such as a Bock, with its relatively low hopping rate, these

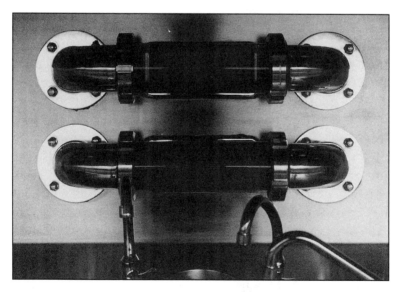

The sight tubes at the Kulmbacher Reichelbräu brewery. Wort from the lauter tun flows through these tubes, and allows the brewmaster to decide when acceptable clarity has been achieved. Photo by Darryl Richman.

may not completely agglomerate into flocs in the boil or settle out during a cold lagering period. Then, a filtering would be needed. Unfortunately, a fine filtering can strip body, flavor, and color out of the beer.

In the end, traditional practice prevails in Germany, reportedly a ninety minute recirculation period followed by an eighty minute lautering process.[38] A sample brewing log from the Bavarian State Brewery at Weihenstephan also indicates an hour and a half recirculation period followed by seventy minutes of sparging.[20] Other breweries may go through shorter recirculations, though all witnessed by the author continue the recirculation of the wort back into the lauter tun until a visual inspection of it shows that it is running clear. Only at that point is the wort then allowed to run into the boil kettle.

A brewmaster might typically make the determination of "clear" wort by the presence of very slight or no haze visible in a two inch (5 cm), or even larger, diameter cylinder. For the purpose of inspection, a piece of glass or plastic tube will be placed in a strategic location in the piping that leads from the lauter tun, with a bright light set behind it. In some cases, the brewer may direct the wort onto the kettle with some fine solids still present. From long experience, though, he knows that this will run completely clear and free of solids within a few minutes of the beginning of the transfer.

Since a decoction mash more completely liquefies and degrades the mash components, producing a wort with a higher sugar concentration after the extended process, it is much easier to slow its outflow, or have the mash "stick," in the lauter tun. Especially for a Bock beer, with its high gravity, slow runoffs can be a problem. It is therefore important to consider the mechanics

The grant is where the outflow from the lauter tun goes. Each faucet takes the outflow from under a different part of the grain bed. Photo by Klaus Koch.

of the lauter tun in its design.

The false bottom of the lauter tun stands off from the bottom of the tun by only 0.3 to 0.6 inches (8 to 15 mm). This minimizes the volume of underletting needed, as well as minimizing the hydrostatic head that, through the suction created, tends to compact the mash bed. The false bottom itself has an open area of no more than 25 percent, and often as little as 6 percent. This slows down the lautering speed, but holds back more of the mash solids, increasing the efficiency of the process. Holes or slits in the false bottom no bigger than 0.031 inches (0.8 mm) in width are recommended to hold back almost all of the smallest particles. These are in greater evidence here, as compared to an infusion mash, due to the vigorous decoction process.[39]

The outflow of the lauter tun is directed to a grant,

or sink. The drain from the grant can be directed back into the lauter tun for recirculation of cloudy wort, or on to the boiling kettle. The usual design of a lauter tun has many separate outflow pipes from different areas under the false bottom. Each pipe will lead to a separate faucet at the grant. The end of each faucet is set very near to the level of the false bottom, minimizing the head and reducing the suction. The arrangement of the grant provides a great deal of flexibility in setting the mash bed. If a particular faucet is running cloudy wort, there is a tear in the bed that can be reset by slowing the lauter speed in that region. A faucet that is delivering a lower gravity wort than other faucets has a significant channel in the bed above its inflow pipe. These problems should be detected and corrected, so as not to produce an inferior product.

Particularly for Bock beers, efficient lautering is critical. If not conducted properly, either the total extract will be very low or else too much volume will be obtained, and an extremely long boil will be required to reduce it. The extract efficiency is inversely proportional to the rate of outflow of wort from the lauter tun. The slower the lautering, the more efficient the process, as long as the mash temperature can be maintained. Patience is a virtue when overseeing the lautering process.

Outflow is measured by the flow per unit of surface area of the mash tun.[39] This makes sense, as this determines a maximum rate of travel for the heavy wort through the mash. This also implies that shallower lauter tuns will operate faster than deep ones, since the wort has to pass through less of the mash to reach the outflow. This concept only applies if the false bottom is equally open across the entire bottom, and there are no

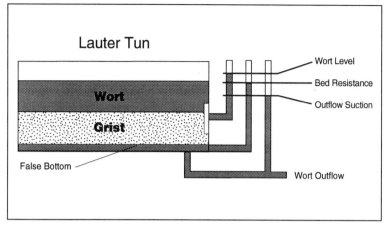

Measuring Pressure and Compaction. After Narziß. [19]

pressure buildups in the drainage.

The classical lauter program, for a decoction mash, begins recirculation at an outflow rate of 0.18 gallons per $f^2$ minute (6.6 L per $m^2$ minute), and rises in four steps over the course of a three hour lautering to 0.33 gallons per $f^2$ minute (12 L per $m^2$ minute). (The square feet ($f^2$) and square meter ($m^2$) measurements are to represent a cross sectional area of flow.) For the home brewer with a lauter tun of 16 inches in diameter, that implies a total surface area of 1.4 square feet; a one foot diameter bucket lauter tun has a total surface area of 0.79 square feet. Once the total surface area is determined, it can be multiplied by the square foot flow rate to obtain a total flow. For the 16-inch lauter tun, that would be a flow rate from 0.25 gallons per minute to 0.46 gallons per minute at the end of the sparge.

Since the outflow rate is determined strictly from the surface area, faster lautering can be obtained with a wide, shallow tun. A tall, narrow tun shape implies a smaller surface area, and a slower overall flow rate. In the traditional German brewhouse, the lauter tun is filled to a depth of no more than 23 inches (55 cm) of malt solids, and no fewer than 10 inches (25 cm).[39]

As lautering continues, the bed of husks and particulates will settle and compress under the pressure of the overlying wort and husks, and from the suction of the draining wort. A comparison of different columns, one taken from the side of the tun, another from underneath the false bottom, and the third from the outflow, can indicate the bed compression and hydrostatic pressure created in the bed from these sources.

This can indicate when the bed has become too compacted to allow efficient flow. Compaction of the bed is remedied by running the mash rakes through the bed. These can be lowered to different depths and cycled around the tun. Cutting the bed is done as often as four times during the course of a long lautering. After cutting the mash, outflow from the tun is recycled back into the tun until it runs clear again.

Sparging is performed as a series of three distinct water additions on top of the mash. These are coordinated with the action of the mash cutting. After the mash is cut, the wort is recycled until the bed is settled. Then the next sparging session begins.

The water for each session may be added on top of the bed all at once. This limits the amount of heat lost in the bed by providing an insulating layer above it. This is important because of the long duration of the lautering process.

The sparge water is added at 167 to 172 degrees F (75 to 78 degrees C). This temperature is chosen because it keeps the wort flowing, but tends to limit the extraction of tannins as the pH of the remaining mash rises. Tannin extraction increases greatly with higher temperatures and a pH over six. The pH rises as more extract is removed. This is because the extract has acidity, and the incoming water will be neutral or alkaline, especially if it has a significant amount of carbonates in it.

The total sparge water used is generally between 1.5 and 2.35 quarts per pound (3.1 to 4.9 L/kg) of malt. The different spargings use different quantities of water. The first is allocated 25 percent of the total. The second sparging is done with 45 percent, and the third with 30 percent.[39] This program is followed in order to balance the need to limit the hydrostatic pressure in the lauter tun, maximizing the columnar flow of extract out of the tun. Both of these allow the lauter to be more efficient, and therefore produce the greatest amount of extract.

If an infusion mash program is followed, it is still wise to lauter slowly, maximizing efficiency. However, because the grist will have maintained more structural integrity throughout the less intensive mash, the bed will not compact as quickly or as completely, and the flow will be quicker. This is evidenced by the usual practice in Britain, where infusion mashing with highly modified malts is the rule. Here, the grain bed is often as deep as three feet. The runoff is much quicker, but the efficiency is generally a few percent lower.

## BOILING

Boiling condenses the volume, sterilizes the wort, increases the wort color, drops haze-forming compounds out of solution, and extracts bitterness and aroma factors from the hops. In a Bock beer, the timing of the boil is very important.

Depending on the volume recovered from the lauter, the boiling time may have to be greatly expanded.

The total of the mash and sparge water will be significantly larger than the intended batch size — from 50 percent to 100 percent larger. Therefore, the specific gravity of the sweet wort collected into the kettle will be correspondingly lower than intended.

In a normal situation, the boil will encompass one and a half to three hours. The wide variation is related to the equipment in use. The equipment will affect the efficiency of the lauter, and therefore, the volume brought into the kettle. The kettle itself affects the situation because its dimensions and heating potential control the evaporation rate. A wide, shallow kettle will have a large surface area to volume ratio, which will increase the evaporation rate. Similarly, a kettle that can deliver more energy to the wort will cause more of it to be boiled off in a given period. Steam heating systems vary, but all deliver more energy than directly fired kettles. It will be necessary for the brewer to discover the evaporation rate of the equipment in use. Without this information, too much volume may be boiled off, or not enough.

The timing is complicated by the need to put the hops in at the right point before the end of the boil. For homebrewers, it is best to allow the boil to go on a bit longer than needed before adding the hops. It is easier to add more water if needed than to adjust for boiling the hops for too long a period.

Wort sterilization is necessary, as with other beer styles, to ensure a successful product. Without this step, all sorts of invaders might have an effect on the final flavor and aroma.

Melanoidin formation is continued in the boil. The intensity of the process is proportional to the time and the gravity of the wort. The color change apparent in a long, high gravity boil is dramatic. A wort with first runnings that are an amber-orange color can take the entire wort to a deep red-brown.

Although a decoction mash produces a wort with significantly fewer high-weight proteins, it does not eliminate them. During the course of this step, these proteins are hurled into each other from the violence of the boil. They stick together, accreting into flocs that fall out of solution. After the addition of the hops, polyphenolic material present in the hops and extracted into the boil can form complexes with any remaining proteins. These may fall out at cooling time, as the cold break. Hops, of course, also add their flavor, aroma, and bitterness characteristics as well.

As described in the beer profile, hop aroma is very limited, to nonexistent, in the dark Bocks. Even in the Maibock style, where the hop character begins to reach some parity with the malt flavors, their presence is usually still restrained.

Hopping rates are not low, however, when viewed in terms of quantity of $\alpha$-acids added to the boil. The reason for this is that the high gravity of the wort inhibits the isomerization of the acids. This isomerization renders them soluble in the wort. Longer boiling makes up for this to some extent, but the effect is counteracted by the wort's increasing density as water is evaporated.

Normally, a brewer might expect to convert 15 to 30 percent of whole flower hops and 30 to 40 percent of hop pellets available alpha acids to their isomerized form.[40] However, at gravities above 1.048 (12 °Plato) the limit gets progressively lower. Rager's formula[46] suggests that a wort of 1.072 (18 °Plato) will have 11 percent less utilization, or 13.5 to 27 percent and 27 to 36 percent respectively.

Generally sixty to ninety minutes of boiling is recommended to get the most bitterness out of the hops. Beyond this time, flavor changes can occur that can reduce the perceived bitterness and lead to muddied flavors.

This is the timing problem mentioned above. The brewer needs to be able to judge accurately the evaporation rate in order to know when the brew is an hour or so from the end.

A long boiling time strips away much of the flavoring and all of the aromatic properties that the hops can bring to the beer. In order to get some of the hop character into a pale Bock, a second, and possibly a third addition of hops is needed at or near the end of the boil.

## COOLING AND PITCHING

Cooling must be rapid and sanitary. Typically, hot break is removed by whirlpooling the hot wort, and cold break is allowed to settle out in a sedimentation tank. In between the two, the wort is cooled and then the yeast is pitched.

Whirlpooling occurs in a cylindrical vessel. The hot wort is pumped into the vessel from a horizontal pipe that connects tangentially to the side, part way up the vessel. This forms a laminar flow with a minimum of turbulence. The bright, bittered wort is then drawn off from a pipe, low on the side of the vessel. Nearly all of the hot break, being less dense than the wort, collects in the center of the vessel.

The wort is then brought to pitching temperature as quickly as possible, usually by a plate-and-frame heat exchanger. The wort flows through the exchanger in one direction and loses its heat to water that passes by in the other, separated from each other by a thin wall of stainless steel. (The warmed water that exits the other end of the exchanger is often used to mash in the next batch of beer.) Pitching temperature varies from about 41 to 50 degrees F (5 to 10 degrees C), with the lower end of this range preferred.

After cooling, the wort is aerated or oxygenated, often by an inline injector. Oxygen saturation in wort occurs at levels of 25 to 35 mg/L, while sterile air saturation results in only about 8 to 9 mg/L of oxygen. These levels are lowered by as much as 15 percent in higher gravity worts, since oxygen is less soluble in them.[23]

While different yeast strains can require differing levels of molecular oxygen, a lack of sufficient oxygen will cause long lag times and increased ester production, both of which are particularly deleterious to beers in the Bock family.

In spite of the greater food value available for the yeast in this concentrated wort, as compared to a standard lager, the brewer can expect only similar levels of growth. This is because the limiting factor is not the availability of wort sugars or FAN, but because the amount of oxygen that can be dissolved into the cold wort is quickly consumed. It might be possible to inject more oxygen into the wort during the lag phase, but as soon as ethanol begins to be produced, it can be oxidized to form undesirable aldehydes.

Once the cooled wort reaches the sedimentation tank, the yeast is pitched. The quantity of yeast used is high, even in terms of lager brewing, because greater quantities of yeast will be needed to ferment the very rich wort. Because the high gravity wort is far from an optimal growth environment for yeast, brewers generally do not reuse the yeast crop from a Bock beer.

Pitching rates for a standard beer (1.048 original

gravity / 12 °Plato) are between 1 and 5 million cells per milliliter of wort. It is expected they will multiply to reach a six to eight times increase in cell count during the growth phase that occurs over the first day or two of the primary fermentation. The pitching rate for Bock beers should be higher to ensure a good start. Fifteen million cells/mL is a good point; levels over 20 million cells/mL are reported to cause excessive sulfury and yeasty flavors to remain in the finished beer.

Some controversy exists regarding whether it is better to filter out the trub completely before pitching, or to let some trub be carried over into the fermenting beer. Trub can form a nutrient source for invading bacteria. Studies have shown, however, that yeast can use sterols contained in the trub to enhance cell wall building during respiration. The Bavarian technique is to allow the yeast to respire on the trub and then separate it before the anaerobic fermentation begins.

The separation from the trub occurs during the twelve to twenty-four hour lag period (respiration phase). Since the yeast is already pitched into the cooled wort,[50] it is critical to do whatever sedimentation can be done before the violent primary fermentation begins. All of the trub will be stirred up after that point.

As a result of the strong protein removal processes that have occurred in a double or triple decoction mash, as much as 16 percent less cold break will be present in the wort, than in a comparable wort produced from an infusion mash.

The beer and active yeast are removed from the sediment tank by the use of a floating outlet.[39] This device allows beer to be drained from just below the surface inside the tank. Once the beer stops running bright, the end has been reached. The remaining beer is discarded along with the cold break.

## PRIMARY FERMENTATION

The primary fermentation continues from the first pitching until the one-third gravity point is reached. This is the point at which the yeast have reduced the beer's gravity to one-third of the wort's original value. For example, if a Doppelbock beer had an original gravity of 1.072 (18 °Plato), the one-third point would be at about 1.024 (6 °Plato). At this point, the high kraeusen has been reached and the yeast is slowing down and building reserves as it enters the stationary phase. The fermentation always takes at least a week, (more likely ten to twelve days), to reach this point.

Typically, the wort cooling phase will bring the temperature to 41 to 45 degrees F (5 to 7 degrees C). As soon as the yeast begins to show signs of fermentation, the temperature of the ferment will rise. The brewer will try to control this rise, slowing it down and keeping it at a low maximum value.

The temperature of the primary fermentation will be held within the 41 to 50 degrees F (5 to 10 degrees C) range, going and staying as low as the brewer believes the yeast will tolerate. The temperature control is a matter of compromise between getting the beer fermented before the yeast flocculates and preventing or limiting unwanted high temperature fermentation by-products like diacetyl and esters.

One program in use is to cool to 41 degrees F (5 degrees C), hold it at that temperature for three days, allow the beer to rise to 48 degrees F (9 degrees C) over the course of the next eight days (a 0.5 degrees C rise every day), and then prevent any further rise in temperature. Signs of fermentation are visible on the second day, and the kraeusen head covers the beer on the third, building up from there. High kraeusen is reached by the fifth day. By the time the twelfth day is reached, the head is falling and the evolution of $CO_2$ has slowed down.

At the end of the primary fermentation, the kraeusen head begins to fall and the beer begins to become bright. Most of the yeast will have fallen to the bottom of the fermenter. There will only be about twice the level present at the original pitching still in suspension.

This is exactly the point at which the yeast will begin to uptake the diacetyl and 2,3 pentanedione that it excreted early in the fermentation. Thus, it is very important that a significant amount of viable and active yeast be retained, or else the beer will end up with a distracting buttery aroma and flavor. Some yeast strains may require help at this point[22] (Weihenstephan 308/Wyeast Munich 2308 is often indicated as such a yeast). This can be accomplished by raising the temperature to ale temperatures, for example, 62 degrees F (17 degrees C) for a day or more, heightening the yeast activity.

## LAGERING

The beer is finished by a long, cold lagering period at or just slightly above freezing temperatures. This period allows the flavors to marry, provides another opportunity for protein-polyphenol complexes (chill haze) to form and sediment out, and for the beer to reach the peak of condition.

Most breweries use pressurized vessels and hold the

pressure to assure the correct carbonation level. Generally, no other carbonation techniques are employed. This is for two reasons. A German brewery, when brewing other beer styles, usually obtains carbonation in beer through the addition of kraeusen, or fermenting young beer. For this reason, no facilities are available to collect $CO_2$ from the primary fermentation, filter it, and inject it back into the finished beer. (Injection of commercially produced $CO_2$ is not allowed if the brewery is to claim adherence to the Reinheitsgebot. The reasoning is that this is not an explicitly mentioned ingredient, even if the same compound gets into the beer naturally in other situations. $CO_2$ captured from the primary can be added back because it was naturally formed during the process of brewing.)

On the other hand, kraeusening is not employed for Bock beers since the fermenting yeast may be stunned by the alcoholic strength and/or high osmotic pressures of the beer to which they are added, as discussed in the section on yeast in the previous chapter. These pressures can cause the yeast to mutate or shut down completely. This can result in new off-flavor problems such as high acetaldehyde or diacetyl levels, as well as provide an opportunity for spoilage bacteria or wild yeast to get a foothold.

The lagering period goes on for a minimum of two months, but can continue for half a year in the case of some specialty Bock beers. During this time, flavor maturation occurs. The lager yeast slows down as the twin forces of high ethanol content and dwindling simple sugars cause it to metabolize other compounds like diacetyl, 2,3 pentanedione, and acetaldehyde. Other redox reactions mediated by the yeast[23] deliver a finished beer that is highly stable.

The yeast will eventually go dormant and fall to the bottom of the vessel, and will have a tendency to drag any remaining haze factors with it. These factors are composed of starches, high weight proteins, and husk and hop polyphenols.

The long lagering period allows the $CO_2$ created by slowing fermentation to stay dissolved in the beer. The lagering tanks are held at a pressure and temperature that enforce the final carbonation levels of the beer. Overpressure is relieved, and any sulfides that might be generated in this last slow fermentative stage are therefore allowed to be purged. What results is a well conditioned, brilliantly clear beer, ready for packaging.

## PACKAGING

At the end of the lagering step, the beer may go through a light polish filtering (at or above 3 µ). This is more likely the case for beer destined to be bottled; kegged beer might not be further handled. The filtering assures that all remaining yeast is removed from the beer. However, filtering is not a replacement for the long lagering period; heavy filtering (under 1 µ) to eliminate haze will remove a percentage of the melanoidins, dextrins and proteins that add mouth feel and create the perception of a rich, luxurious product.

Every precaution must be taken at this point to prevent any oxygen from getting into the beer. The filtering process requires extreme care to avoid reintroducing oxygen. As described in the section on melanoidins in the last chapter, these compounds will stabilize the beer and assure a long shelf life only if they make it into the final product in an unoxidized (reduced) state. If they do become oxidized, they can transfer this oxidation on to alcohols, forming aldehydes that will color and age the beer.

It is important for craft brewers who want to bottle to understand the limitations of this form of packaging. A long lagering reduces the quantity and viability of the yeast in suspension, which will cause very slow carbonation. Therefore, the beer should be primed and bottled after a shortened lagering period of no more than two months. The beer, once bottled, should be allowed to warm to primary fermentation temperatures for one or two weeks until carbonation is complete. It should then go through a subsequent lagering to clear and finish before serving.

Priming can be accomplished with unfermented wort or corn sugar (if the brewer is not concerned about the Reinheigsgebot). To obtain 2.1 to 2.3 volumes of $CO_2$ (0.41 to 0.45 g $CO_2$ / 100 g beer), wort should be added so that there are an additional 0.0038 to 0.0042 specific gravity points per gallon to five gallons of beer, 5 x 0.0038 → 0.019, or one gallon at 1.019 (4.75° Plato). This is a very diluted wort, and the extra volume it brings will unneccessarily dilute the beer. Adding one-half gallon of wort of specific gravity 1.038 (9.5° Plato) — twice the strength — will have the same effect.

Instead of saved wort, dry malt extract could be used. For five gallons (19 L) of beer, 0.43 to 0.47 pounds (195 to 214 g) dry malt added to enough water, boiled, cooled, and racked off of the trub will produce the needed extract. To use corn sugar (glucose), use 0.32 to 0.35 pounds (145 to 159 g) for each five gallons (19 L).

# 5

# Recipes

As detailed in previous chapters, brewing a quality Bock beer requires a great deal of effort and care. The recipes given here reflect this fact, and are time-consuming to execute. World class Bock beers can be produced in the craft environment; some of the best commercial varieties are made in small, very traditional breweries without exceptional facilities.

Perhaps the greatest leap of faith required is to believe that after a very long boil, the large volume will be reduced to the right size, and the color and gravity will come up. That doesn't seem like such a wide chasm to cross.

The recipes are given in two sizes: five U.S. gallons and one U.S. barrel (thirty-one gallons). The larger is strictly a scaled up version of the smaller, since the changes in the variables of differently sized production plants can only be predicted by the brewer for specific equipment. This may actually assist the professional brewer who wants to try pilot batches before proceeding on to full scale. In such a situation, the brewer will know from experience how to adjust a recipe for particular equipment.

The color of the final beer cannot be directly predicted from the color of the malts. Fix[51] has stated why this is generally the case: malt color contribution is nonlinear. Even so, these recipes were formulated with this problem in mind. Please note, though, that the reduction by long boil causes an additional darkening, which the literature does not reveal a way to measure. Experience shows that the color will come up to an appropriate level.

The extract rate assumptions here play an important role in the reader's ability to use the recipes. There is much confusion in the amateur literature about extract measurements. Two systems have come into wide use, and each can indicate a "percent yield" figure. In discussing these approaches, I use *yield* to refer to a percentage value and *extract* to indicate a gravity value.

One system, adopted from professional use, measures yield as a percentage of the dry weight of the original malt, as described in the chapter on materials. This includes the weight of husks and protein material that is either not soluble or drops out in the break matter, meaning that only about 80 percent of the original pale malt can actually be extracted as sugars and dextrins, under even the best of circumstances (which can often only be achieved in a laboratory with an extremely fine milling and filtering through filter paper). As the malt color goes up, this maximum (or *theoretical*) yield goes down.

Another, perhaps more popular, technique arises from the ease and directness of measuring it in the craft environment. This is based on measuring the original gravity of the beer and the volume of beer produced, then dividing back by the number of pounds of malt that went into its production. This yields a value in units of *specific gravity points* x *gallons of beer / pounds of malt.* If a theoretical maximum yield of 80 percent of the malt weight results in a wort with 36 points of extract x gallons/pound, then this number represents 100 percent of the available yield. Therefore, an extract of 30 points x gallons/pound is 30/36ths, or 83.25 percent *system yield.*

There are advantages to each side. Since the theoretical yield system takes into account all of the weight of the original malt, it leads to direct computation of material costs. The system's extract, on the other hand, is immediately and simply computed, and the yield figure is then easily obtained. It can also be quickly used to to compare and adjust recipes that originate from other breweries.

The conversion between theoretical yield and the system's extract is straightforward. Dr. George Fix explains that Plato's table shows that 31 pounds of extract in a barrel (1 pound per gallon) has a specific gravity of 1.046.[49] From this, we can take the theoretical yield (Y) and get the system extract (E) in point gallons per pound:

$$E = 0.463 \times Y, \text{ and, therefore, } Y = 2.16 \times E$$

These recipes assume a 67 percent theoretical yield or a system extract of 30 point gallons per pound (which works out to an 83 percent system yield). These seem to be average numbers achievable in craft-breweries. If this does not match your results on your system, the adjustment down or up to the grist to obtain the correct extract should not be far; use the ratio of your system yield to the assumed system yield (30 point gallons per pound) as a multiplier. Also, such adjustment should not affect the color calculations significantly. Since any changes needed will be small, the recipe should still produce a correctly colored beer.

Hop utilization is always important. There are three considerations when deciding on a hopping schedule. Two of them have to do with bittering, and one with flavor and aroma.

The first issue deals with bittering units. The bittering value of hops in brewing is usually given in one of two forms. There are IBUs (International Bittering Units, in mg of iso-α-acids/L of beer) or AAUs (Alpha Acid Units, in hundredths of ounces of α-acids or, equivalently, ounce-percentage of α-acids. These have also come to be referred to as HBUs or Homebrew Bittering Units). The former is a measurement of bittering content in beer, while the latter is a measurement of bittering potential in hops.

The professional brewer may send beer to a lab for a thorough analysis, and use the IBU results as feedback into the process. The craft-brewer has no such recourse. The feedback here is based on the potential bittering (AAUs). The actual bitterness transferred to the beer is an indirect result of the AAUs used. Usually a craft-brewer will estimate the relationship between AAUs going into the process and likely IBU content of the product, via a bittering function.

Another difference is that IBU units are volume independent: 25 IBUs means the same level of bitterness regardless of the volume of beer that was produced. Five AAUs implies a fixed amount of hops, and therefore a varying amount of bitterness in differently sized batches.

These two different measurements are related by a hop bittering function. This function is affected by the length of boil, boiling temperature, turbulence of the boil, the physical availability of the hop resins that contain the α-acids, and the specific gravity of the wort the hops are boiled in. These variables are generally lumped together into a single utilization percentage. Suggested reading on this topic is Jackie Rager's article, "Calculating Hop Bitterness in Beer."[46]

For these recipes, a 25 percent utilization for whole hops and 30 percent for hop pellets will be used. The low end of the hop quantity range in the recipes is for hop pellets with an assumed 5 percent α-acid content; the high value is for hop flowers with 4 percent. (Higher quantities of hops are required when the α-acid content and/or the utilization rate is lower.) These are chosen to allow a range of typical values. Of course, the hops degrade over time, and old hops will not have the bittering power of fresh hops; hops exposed to the air and/or not refrigerated or frozen will degrade far more quickly than adequately protected hops.

The extract recipes call for significant amounts of "adjunct" malts, for several reasons. The quality of extracts can be uncertain. If substantial quantities of refined sugars have been added they will dilute the protein and dextrin content, reducing mouthfeel and lowering the final gravity, which are the opposites of the characteristics expected from Bock beers. The change in wort sugar make up can also affect the balance of flavors that result from the melanoidin formation process.

Since large quantities of extract are used, it is important to employ as large a boil as possible. The recipes assume that a two-gallon boil is used (and to do this, a four-gallon pot will be needed). This is the minimum volume advisable: if possible a full five-gallon boil, or as close as can be achieved, is optimum.

When adding the extract to the water, be sure to remove or turn down the heat first to prevent the extract from scorching and burning on the bottom. Only once it is dissolved completely should the heat be turned up again.

If a full-volume boil is used, the hopping rates from the five-gallon infusion or decoction batches should be used. If a volume between two and five gallons is used, the hopping rate can be determined by interpolating between the extract and infusion hopping rates. This will compensate for the lowered gravity in the boil and the resulting higher hop utilization.[46]

The adjunct malts are used by crushing them, adding them to the water intended for use in the boil, and gradually heating to 150 to 160 degrees F (65 to 71 degrees C), holding it at the temperature for at least half an hour; an hour is better. Afterwards, the remaining grist is removed, either by straining the wort or by having put the malt into a grain bag before starting. The fastidious brewer will use a grain bag and a colander to attempt to sparge more of the extract from the malt.[35]

The yeast used must be of high quality and high viability to produce the really clean lager character that is a hallmark of this style. A large amount of pitching yeast is critical; the pitching should be made from at least one ounce (30 mL) of thick yeast slurry for each gallon (3.785 L) of wort.

Therefore, homebrewers will find dry "lager" yeasts unsatisfactory, and the liquid pouches of yeast insufficient. Dry yeast packages rarely contain real *S. uvarum* cultures;[52] it apparently does not endure the drying process well. The commercially available liquid yeast pouches contain far too little yeast and growth medium to reach the needed level of yeast cells and must be further propagated in a starter.

In order to grow up enough yeast to pitch into a five-gallon batch, a starter of between half and one gallon is needed (three to six gallons per barrel). Adding such a large starter could have a significant effect on the outcome of the beer, and because of that, a concentrating technique should be used. First, the viable yeast culture is pitched into a one-quart, aerated starter, of gravity between 1.020 and 1.040 (5 to 10 °Plato) and allowed to ferment at 68 degrees F (20 degrees C) for about two or three days until the yeast flocculates out.

The clear liquid above is poured off and as much as a gallon of aerated wort is added. For larger batch sizes, additional propagation steps are required. To reach the pitching yeast for one barrel, this gallon step should then be pitched into five gallons.

The last propagation step is also allowed to ferment out. The temperature is gradually reduced to the pitching temperature 41 to 50 degrees F (5 to 10 degrees C). Several hours before pitching, the liquid is again poured off and a pint of wort (half gallon per barrel), is added at pitching temperature. At pitching, this is swirled to suspend all of the yeast and added to the wort at or just before the pint (half gallon) reaches high kraeusen.

An alternative technique that uses a lower pitching rate, but requires more careful temperature control, is to grow up the starter in a volume of a quart to a half gallon for a five-gallon batch (1.5 to 3 gallons per barrel), maintaining 68 degrees F (20 degrees C). This is pitched, when high kraeusen is reached, into the wort at the same temperature. The beer is gradually reduced in temperature to the primary fermentation range over the course of two days.

This is risky for several reasons. If cooling is done too slowly, the yeast will take off very fast, perhaps creating unwanted esters and higher initial levels of diacetyl. If the cooling is too quick, the yeast may be shocked or flocculate too quickly, causing high diacetyl levels to remain in the finished product. It may also be difficult to go through the sedimentation step while trying to attemperate the beer.

## HEILIGE GEIST HELLES BOCK

You'll find this to be a particularly substantial ghost. With a color of 6 °SRM (15 °EBC) for the all-grain versions and 8 °SRM (20 °EBC) for the extract, these beers turn out to be a deep gold to light amber color.

The high original gravity of 1.066 (16.5 °Plato), places this beer solidly in the Bock range. As a result, it will have a rich, malty flavor and aroma. The use, even in the extract recipe, of a large quantity of Munich and caramel malts provides these essential malt characteristics to the finished beer. Without it, the beer will be big and flabby, flat and without distinguishing character and elegance.

The hopping level is light at 28 IBUs, and will be perceived by the drinker as being even lighter than that number would imply in a normal gravity beer.

All water used in this recipe should be low in carbonates. In fact, a soft, low mineral content water accented by as much as 50 mg/L of calcium is ideal. If you have carbonate water, boil and decant or use other techniques as described in the section on water treatment to remove it, especially for the sparge.

For all-grain, five-gallon sized batch mashes, the dough-in should be made with 3.5 gallons (13.25 L). For infusion mashes, use five gallons (19 L) for sparging; for decoction, use 5.5 to 6 gallons (21 to 23 L). The larger quantity in part makes up for the volume boiled off in a double decoction. For one-barrel batches, use 21.7 gallons (0.82 hL) for dough-in. Use either one barrel (1.17 hL) when decocting, or thirty-four to thirty-seven gallons (1.29 to 1.41 hL) when infusing, as sparge liquor.

When following the decoction program, be sure to pull more than a third of the thick mash, and add it back slowly until the next temperature rest is reached. If slightly higher temperatures are reached, no great harm will come; if the rests are well over shot, the mash can be thinned with cold water. The only difficult problem is substantially under-shooting the mark. Take careful notes! Once this information is obtained, subsequent decoctions will be easy.

To employ infusion, consider following the rest mash temperature program. The long times spent at each rest seem to be more than is needed to obtain proteolysis and saccharification. It is likely that a thirty- to sixty-minute protein rest and an hour to and hour and one half of sugar rest should be sufficient. Since the subsequent grain bed will have more structure than in decoction, there is always the temptation to lauter quickly. Resist it as much as is possible, and take the runoff slowly. This will allow the wort to clear more quickly and reduce recirculation times, making it more efficient (for example, more extract obtained with less sparge water).

Unless it is known how much will be boiled off in an hour, all grain brewers should boil the volume down to 110 to 120 percent of the final volume before adding the bittering hops. Be careful; try not to boil your hops more than an hour and a half. It is better to add water toward the end of the boil if your volume will be too low. The flavoring hops should be added in the last ten minutes of the boil.

## HEILIGE GEIST HELLES BOCK

| Extract | Infusion | | Decoction | |
|---|---|---|---|---|
| 5 gallons | 5 gallons | 1 barrel | 5 gallons | 1 barrel |
| **Lager Malt** | | | | |
| – | 5.25 lb. | 32.5 lb. | 5.5 lb. | 34.1 lb. |
| – | 2.4 kg. | 14.8 kg. | 2.4 kg. | 15.5 kg. |
| **Munich Malt** | | | | |
| 1.5 lb. | 5 lb. | 31 lb. | 5.5 lb. | 34.1 lb. |
| 0.7 kg. | 2.3 kg. | 14.1 kg. | 2.5 kg. | 15.5 kg. |
| **Pale Caramel Malt** | | | | |
| 1.5 lb. | 1 lb. | 6.2 lb. | – | – |
| 0.7 kg. | 0.45 kg. | 2.8 kg. | – | – |
| **Dark Caramel Malt** | | | | |
| – | – | – | – | – |
| **Chocolate Malt** | | | | |
| – | – | – | – | – |
| **Pale Malt Syrup** | | | | |
| 6.6 lb. | – | – | – | – |
| 3 kg. | – | – | – | – |
| **Pale Dry Malt Extract** | | | | |
| 0.5 lb. | – | – | – | – |
| 0.23 kg. | – | – | – | – |

HOPPING SCHEDULE

**Bittering Hops**

| | | | | |
|---|---|---|---|---|
| 2.75-4.25 oz. | 1.25-1.9 oz. | 7.75-11.75 oz. | 1.25-1.9 oz. | 7.75-11.75 oz. |
| 78-120 gm. | 35-54 gm. | 220-333 gm. | 35-54 gm. | 220-333 gm. |
| 13.75-17 AAU | 6.25-7.6 AAU | 38.75-47 AAU | 6.25-7.6 AAU | 38.75-47 AAU |

**Flavoring Hops**

| | | | | |
|---|---|---|---|---|
| 0.75 oz. | 0.5 oz. | 3.1 oz. | 0.5 oz. | 3.1 oz. |
| 21 gm. | 14 gm. | 88 gm. | 14 gm. | 88 gm. |

**Aroma Hops**

| | | | | |
|---|---|---|---|---|
| – | – | – | – | – |

# KEINBECKER MAIBOCK

The outstanding example of this style that I know is Einbecker Maibock. This is not an Einbecker, but it is close; it is rich and malty, flowery with noble hop aroma and a lasting bitterness. This recipe will put you near to that goal with its 35 IBUs of bitterness, and slightly darker color that the real Einbecker has 8 °SRM (20 °EBC). A little extra oomph is provided in the original gravity of 1.070 (17.5 °Plato).

The notes for making the *Heilige Geist* Helles Bock should be your guide here as well. Use only the finest, freshest hops for flavor and aromatic needs. Add the aroma hops when you turn off the heat at the end of the boil.

# KEINBECKER MAIBOCK

| Extract | Infusion | | Decoction | |
|---|---|---|---|---|
| 5 gallons | 5 gallons | 1 barrel | 5 gallons | 1 barrel |
| **Lager Malt** | | | | |
| – | 5.5 lb. | 34.1 lb. | 5.5 lb. | 34.1 lb. |
| – | 2.5 kg. | 15.5 kg. | 2.5 kg. | 15.5 kg. |
| **Munich Malt** | | | | |
| 1.5 lb. | 5.5 lb. | 34.1 lb. | 6.25 lb. | 38.75 lb. |
| 0.7 kg. | 2.5 kg. | 15.5 kg. | 2.8 kg. | 17.6 kg. |
| **Pale Caramel Malt** | | | | |
| 1.5 lb. | 1 lb. | 6.2 lb. | – | – |
| 0.7 kg. | 0.45 kg. | 2.8 kg. | – | – |
| **Dark Caramel Malt** | | | | |
| – | – | – | – | – |
| **Chocolate Malt** | | | | |
| – | – | – | – | – |
| **Pale Malt Syrup** | | | | |
| 6.6 lb. | – | – | – | – |
| 3 kg. | – | – | – | – |
| **Pale Dry Malt Extract** | | | | |
| 0.5 lb. | – | – | – | – |
| 0.23 kg. | – | – | – | – |

## HOPPING SCHEDULE

**Bittering Hops**

| | | | | |
|---|---|---|---|---|
| 2.75-4.25 oz. | 1.5-2.4 oz. | 9.3-14.9 oz. | 1.5-2.4 oz. | 9.3-14.9 oz. |
| 78-120 gm. | 43-68 gm. | 264-422 gm. | 43-68 gm. | 264-422 gm. |
| 13.75-17 AAU | 7.5-9.6 AAU | 46.5-60 AAU | 7.5-9.6 AAU | 46.5-60 AAU |

**Flavoring Hops**

| | | | | |
|---|---|---|---|---|
| 1 oz. | 0.75 oz. | 4.6 oz. | 0.75 oz. | 4.6 oz. |
| 28 gm. | 21 gm. | 130 gm. | 21 gm. | 130 gm. |

**Aroma Hops**

| | | | | |
|---|---|---|---|---|
| 0.75 oz. | 0.5 oz. | 3.1 oz. | 0.5 oz. | 3.1 oz. |
| 21 gm. | 14 gm. | 88 gm. | 14 gm. | 88 gm. |

## ELIAS PICHLER DUNKLES BOCK

This Dunkles Bock is named for the second brew-master of the Hofbräuhaus' Braunbrauerei. It was his journey south to Munich and ability to synthesize his knowledge with the experience of his peers in Bavaria that produced the archetype of the style.

This beer is dark at 22 °SRM (57 °EBC) but not black or opaque. Right in the Bock classification for strength at 1.068 original gravity (17 °Plato), it has a very low bitterness of 24 IBUs. In spite of this low bitterness, it is not as sweet as its Helles cousins, because the high melanoidin content gives the beer a drier finish.

The notes from the Heilige Geist recipe apply here as well, except that the water should have the typical Munich carbonate hardness for the mash; a triple decoction or step infusion program should be followed.

The sparge water should be moderated in its carbonate content, as described in the water section of chapter 3. If not, the pH of the mash bed will rise above 6.0, which will extract polyphenols and create an unwanted harshness in the finished beer.[35] Therefore, water with a low carbonate ion content is preferred for sparging.

For extract brewers, carbonate water should be employed for the boil. This will increase color and emphasize what little hops are present. The carbonate content is not important in the water used to top up to five gallons that is added after the boil.

# ELIAS PICHLER DUNKLES BOCK

| Extract | Infusion | | Decoction | |
|---|---|---|---|---|
| 5 gallons | 5 gallons | 1 barrel | 5 gallons | 1 barrel |
| **Lager Malt** | | | | |
| – | 1 lb. | 6.2 lb. | 1 lb. | 6.2 lb. |
| – | 0.45 kg. | 2.8 kg. | 0.45 kg. | 2.8 kg. |
| **Munich Malt** | | | | |
| 1 lb. | 9.5 lb. | 58.9 lb. | 9.5 lb. | 58.9 lb. |
| 0.45 kg. | 4.3 kg. | 26.8 kg. | 4.3 kg. | 26.8 kg. |
| **Pale Caramel Malt** | | | | |
| 1 lb. | – | – | 0.5 lb. | 3.1 lb. |
| 0.45 kg. | – | – | 0.28 kg. | 1.4 kg. |
| **Dark Caramel Malt** | | | | |
| 1 lb. | 1 lb. | 6.2 lb. | 0.5 lb. | 3.1 lb. |
| 0.45 kg. | 0.45 kg. | 2.8 kg. | 0.23 kg. | 1.4 kg. |
| **Chocolate Malt** | | | | |
| 2 oz. | 2 oz. | 0.75 lb. | 2 oz. | 0.75 lb. |
| 57 gm. | 57 gm. | 0.34 kg. | 57 gm. | 0.34 kg. |
| **Pale Malt Syrup** | | | | |
| 6.6 lb. | – | – | – | – |
| 3 kg. | – | – | – | – |
| **Pale Dry Malt Extract** | | | | |
| 0.5 lb. | – | – | – | – |
| 0.23 kg. | – | – | – | – |

## HOPPING SCHEDULE

| | | | | |
|---|---|---|---|---|
| **Bittering Hops** | | | | |
| 2.75-4.25 oz. | 1.1-1.75 oz. | 6.8-10.85 oz. | 1.1-1.75 oz. | 6.8-10.85 oz. |
| 78-120 gm. | 31-50 gm. | 193-308 gm. | 31-50 gm. | 193-308 gm. |
| 13.75-17 AAU | 5.5-7 AAU | 34-43 AAU | 5.5-7 AAU | 34-43 AAU |
| **Flavoring Hops** | | | | |
| 0.5 oz. | 0.25 oz. | 1.5 oz. | 0.25 oz. | 1.5 oz. |
| 14 gm. | 7 gm. | 43 gm. | 7 gm. | 43 gm. |
| **Aroma Hops** | | | | |
| – | – | – | – | – |

# PLACATOR DOPPELBOCK

The tradition of naming Doppelbocks with a trailing -*ator* is nothing more than that — a tradition. There is no requirement in law for this appellation, and there are many Doppelbocks that do not follow tradition. It does, however, lead the brewer to the making of lists that go something like this: Debilitator, Escalator, Elevator, Pocket Calculator (for the engineering types), Mercator, Inebriator, Facilitator (a gift for President Clinton), Manipulator, Alternator, Generator (for the motorheads of your acquaintance), In-Sink-Erator®, See you lator, Accelerator, Resuscitator, Integrator (for the math whiz or the socially conscious), Alligator, Discombobulator, Humiliator (for that Saxon Knight), Prevaricator, Antidisestablishmentarianator, ... well, you get the idea.

*"The secret to a great Bock beer is that the drinker shouldn't notice its strength until he gets up from the table"*
— a Bavarian Brewmaster

The one to have when you're only having half. With an original gravity of 1.074 (18.5 °Plato), and a final gravity of approximately 1.020 (5 °Plato), this beer has an alcohol level of 6.9 percent v/v (5.5 percent w/v). Yet, with a clean lager yeast, the alcohol is in tune with the other flavors of the beer.

Brewing techniques are as above, in the Dunkles Bock recipe. This recipe has 25 IBUs, contributing only a low level of background bitterness. Therefore, it relies heavily on melanoidin production for the dryness of the resulting beer. This is emphasized by the estimated color of 24 °SRM (62 °EBC).

121

# PLACATOR DOPPELBOCK

| Extract | Infusion | | Decoction | |
|---|---|---|---|---|
| 5 gallons | 5 gallons | 1 barrel | 5 gallons | 1 barrel |
| **Lager Malt** | | | | |
| – | 1.5 lb. | 9.3 lb. | 1.5 lb. | 9.3 lb. |
| – | 0.7 kg. | 4.2 kg. | 0.7 kg. | 4.2 kg. |
| **Munich Malt** | | | | |
| 1.5 lb. | 10.25 lb. | 63.5 lb. | 10.25 lb. | 63.5 lb. |
| 0.7 kg. | 4.7 kg. | 28.9 kg. | 4.7 kg. | 28.9 kg. |
| **Pale Caramel Malt** | | | | |
| 1 lb. | – | – | 0.5 lb. | 3.1 lb. |
| 0.45 kg. | – | – | 0.23 kg. | 1.4 kg. |
| **Dark Caramel Malt** | | | | |
| 1 lb. | 1 lb. | 6.2 lb. | 0.5 lb. | 3.1 lb. |
| 0.45 kg. | 0.45 kg. | 2.8 kg. | 0.23 kg. | 1.4 kg. |
| **Chocolate Malt** | | | | |
| 2 oz. | 2 oz. | 0.75 lb. | 2 oz. | 0.75 lb. |
| 57 gm. | 57 gm. | 0.34 kg. | 57 gm. | 0.34 kg. |
| **Pale Malt Syrup** | | | | |
| 6.6 lb. | – | – | – | – |
| 3 kg. | – | – | – | – |
| **Pale Dry Malt Extract** | | | | |
| 1 lb. | – | – | – | – |
| 0.45 kg. | – | – | – | – |

## HOPPING SCHEDULE

| **Bittering Hops** | | | | |
|---|---|---|---|---|
| 3.25-4.75 oz. | 1.25-1.9 oz. | 7.75-11.75 oz. | 1.25-1.9 oz. | 7.75-11.75 oz. |
| 92-135 gm. | 35-54 gm. | 220-333 gm. | 35-54 gm. | 220-333 gm. |
| 16.25-19 AAU | 6.25-7.6 AAU | 38.75-108 AAU | 6.25-7.6 AAU | 38.75-108 AAU |
| **Flavoring Hops** | | | | |
| 0.5 oz. | 0.25 oz. | 1.5 oz. | 0.25 oz. | 1.5 oz. |
| 14 gm. | 7 gm. | 43 gm. | 7 gm. | 43 gm. |
| **Aroma Hops** | | | | |
| – | – | – | – | – |

# ALTES BOCK

Here are two recipes for recreations of Bierstadt Einbecker Bier and Ainpoeckisches Pier. I have not attempted to provide a recipe for the monkish Sankt-Vater-Bier because it would be especially difficult to get the low attenuation rates with modern yeasts, and the result would likely have very limited flavor and drinkability.

Getting the low attenuation rates for these two beers is difficult. Modern malts are highly modified and carefully kilned compared to what would have been available four to six hundred years ago, producing more fermentable worts, more readily.

Our modern mashing techniques and tools will add to the high yield in comparison to the primitive measurements available to the ancients. They could only reliably tell 32 degrees F, 98 degrees F, and 212 degrees F (0 degrees C, 37 degrees C, and 100 degrees C, respectively). Other estimation techniques can vary greatly according to the ambient temperature and humidity. (This is likely the origin of decoction mashing, which only requires being able to measure volume and detect blood and boiling temperatures. Modern decoction fancifies the procedure with its decoct rests, in order to get the last drop of extract possible.)

Consider a mashing program (either decoction or step infusion) beginning with 100 degrees F (38 degrees C) water, 1.25 quarts per pound of malt (2.6 liters per kilogram). Rest for an hour to an hour and a quarter. Step up to about 135 degrees F (57 degrees C), rest about forty-five minutes. Then step up again to 162 degrees F (72 degrees C) for thirty minutes.

Remember, these beers would have been at least

hazy, if not very cloudy, with starch and protein and tannin. This is because lautering techniques were also minimal and a lot of mash solids would have been carried over into the boil. For greater realism, do not recirculate, but run off directly into the kettle.

Sparge with a similar amount of water to that used in the mash. Add it in three equal parts, the first and third at boiling temperatures, and the middle at 100 degrees F (38 degrees C). Lautering and sparging work by first draining the lauter tun of the mash wort. Then the first portion sparge water is added, mixed with the mash, and drained. Repeat for the second and third sparges. Although the total water used is 2.5 quarts per pound of malt (5.6 liters per kilogram), not all of it will be retrieved as wort. Roughly 15 to 20 percent will stay with the grains.

(This inefficient sparging technique leaves behind substantial amounts of extract. Perhaps a small beer was made with additional alternating temperature sparges. A similar process is described in *Scotch Ale* by Greg Noonan.)[53]

The recipes below assume that the brewer will achieve a system extract of twenty-four specific gravity points in a gallon of wort per pound of malt (52 percent theoretical yield, or 67 percent system yield), because of this inefficiency. One might be able to sparge out the remaining sugars and make half as much more (e.g., 2.5 gallons from a five-gallon batch of Altes Bock) of a small lager with a gravity of perhaps 1.036 (9 °Plato).

A part of the secret to low attenuation rates, besides nonculture yeast, is a long, concentrated boil. This causes caramelization and melanoidin formation, which locks up sugars and prevents the yeast from being able to ferment them. The recipes below should yield about 135 percent of the intended batch size into the kettle, which is to be boiled down over two to three hours.

The main fermentation should be carried out by a good performing ale yeast. The temperature should be in the range of about 50 to 55 degrees F (10 to 13 degrees C). Such a low temperature will cause many ale strains to go dormant and thus fail to ferment the wort; experiment with a starter first. One yeast that has this low temperature tolerance is Wyeast 1056. This temperature range will cause the yeast to proceed very slowly; it may take three weeks to finish.

If more realism is wanted, lactic acid bacteria (Pediococcus and Lactobacillus strains) can be added. They should be added at the start of fermentation. However, once these have been added, the beer has a limited shelf life; it will continue to grow more acidic as time progresses. (Suggested reading on this subject is Jean-Xavier Guinard's *Lambic*.)[24]

Alternatively, dosing the finished beer with a few hundred to up to two thousand mg/L of food grade lactic acid will give a mild to strong tartness. One can add the acid with a pipette to a pint of beer in order to determine a level of "pleasant acidity," and then dose the entire batch to match. This provides greater control over the final product, but the character it achieves is a bit one-dimensional; lactic acid bacteria generate other by-products. In either case, the bitterness levels should be inversely proportional to the lactic acid concentration, for the most pleasing results.

Lagering should be carried out for at least six weeks; the more time, the better up to about three months. (Note the caution above regarding any lactic bacteria.) This should be done at 35 to 45 degrees F (2 to 7 degrees C).

Since all of these beers would have been packaged in wooden barrels, lower levels of carbonation would be the rule here. A barrel has a limited ability to hold pressure, and during aging, the pressure would gradually bleed off. Consider using less than two volumes of $CO_2$ (0.39g $CO_2$/100g beer).

These recipes are certainly not the final word on the subject. Much is unknown about the brewing process from this era and locale. Instead, consider these as jumping off points, and let your imagination run free.

## BIERSTADT EINBECKER BIER

This is a recipe for a medium amber beer of about 12 to 14 °SRM (30 to 35 °EBC), with an original gravity of 1.066 (16.5 °Plato). Because of low attenuation, the final gravity should be about 1.022 (5.5 °Plato), resulting in an apparent attenuation of 66 percent and an alcohol level of 4.9 percent w/v (6.2 percent v/v).

Bitterness is higher, at 38 IBUs, than in more modern beers. The perception of bitterness will increase as more of the old fashioned techniques are employed, which result in carrying more polyphenols over into the beer. The brewer may want to moderate this level of bitterness, especially if any of the acidifying techniques discussed above are used.

Soft water should be used in this recipe; the softer, the better. However, the water could be adjusted to about 50 mg/L of calcium.

# BIERSTADT EINBECKER BIER

| Extract | Infusion | | Decoction | |
|---|---|---|---|---|
| 5 gallons | 5 gallons | 1 barrel | 5 gallons | 1 barrel |
| **Lager Malt** | | | | |
| – | 3.5 lb. | 21.7 lb. | 4.5 lb. | 27.9 lb. |
| – | 1.6 kg. | 9.9 kg. | 2 kg. | 12.7 kg. |
| **Munich Malt** | | | | |
| 2 lb. | 11 lb. | 68.2 lb. | 10 lb. | 62 lb. |
| 0.9 kg. | 5 kg. | 31 kg. | 4.5 kg. | 28.2 kg. |
| **Pale Caramel Malt** | | | | |
| – | – | – | – | – |
| **Dark Caramel Malt** | | | | |
| – | – | – | – | – |
| **Chocolate Malt** | | | | |
| 2 oz. | 2 oz. | 0.75 lb. | 2 oz. | 0.75 lb. |
| 57 gm. | 57 gm. | 0.34 kg. | 57 gm. | 0.34 kg. |
| **Pale Malt Syrup** | | | | |
| 6.6 lb. | – | – | – | – |
| 3 kg. | | | | |
| **Pale Dry Malt Extract** | | | | |
| 1 lb. | – | – | – | – |
| 0.45 kg. | – | – | – | – |

## HOPPING SCHEDULE

| **Bittering Hops** | | | | |
|---|---|---|---|---|
| 3-4.4 oz. | 1.5-2.25 oz. | 9.3-14 oz. | 1.5-2.25 oz. | 9.3-14 oz. |
| 85-125 gm. | 42.5-63.8 gm. | 264-370 gm. | 42.5-63.8 gm. | 264-370 gm. |
| 15-17.6 AAU | 7.5-9 AAU1 | 46.5-56 AAU | 7.5-9 AAU | 46.5-56 AAU |
| **Flavoring Hops** | | | | |
| 2.5-4 oz. | 1.33-2 oz. | 8.25-12.4 oz. | 1.33-2 oz. | 8.25-12.4 oz. |
| 71-113 gm. | 38-57 gm. | 234-352 gm. | 38-57 gm. | 234-352 gm. |
| **Aroma Hops** | | | | |
| 3-4 oz. | 2 oz. | 12.4 oz. | 2 oz. | 12.4 oz. |
| 85-113 gm. | 57 gm. | 352 gm. | 57 gm. | 352 gm. |

*127*

## AINPOECKISCHES PIER

Here is an attempt to recreate the output of the München Braunbierbrauerei. The result is a deep brown color with red highlights; about 25 to 30 °SRM (66 to 78 °EBC). The original gravity of 1.066 (16.5 °Plato) is the same as the Einbecker beer above, with a similar final gravity of 1.022 (5.5 °Plato).

Bitterness is reduced to 25 IBUs. Acidity, if added, should be at the low end of the scale.

Carbonate water should be used as described in Chapter 3. Sparging may be conducted with carbonate water, because the amount used is limited. Even so, this will result in some quantity of polyphenols being extracted. The drying effect will help to balance the beer, but it will be less smooth because of it. (Remember, we are speaking of a historical product; see Chapter 2.)

# AINPOECKISCHES PIER

| Extract | Infusion | | Decoction | |
|---|---|---|---|---|
| 5 gallons | 5 gallons | 1 barrel | 5 gallons | 1 barrel |
| **Lager Malt** | | | | |
| – | – | – | 1.5 lb. | 9.3 lb. |
| – | – | – | 0.68 kg. | 4.2 kg. |
| **Munich Malt** | | | | |
| 1.5 lb. | 14 lb. | 86.8 lb. | 12.5 lb. | 77.5 lb. |
| 0.68 kg. | 6.4 kg. | 39.5 kg. | 5.7 kg. | 35.2 kg. |
| **Pale Caramel Malt** | | | | |
| – | – | – | – | – |
| **Dark Caramel Malt** | | | | |
| 1.25 lb. | 1 lb. | 6.2 lb. | 1 lb. | 6.2 lb. |
| 0.57 kg. | 0.45 kg. | 2.8 kg. | 0.45 kg. | 2.8 kg. |
| **Chocolate Malt** | | | | |
| 3 oz. | 3 oz. | 1.16 lb. | 3 oz. | 1.16 lb. |
| 85 gm. | 85 gm. | 0.53 kg. | 85 gm. | 0.53 kg. |
| **Pale Malt Syrup** | | | | |
| 6.6 lb. | – | – | – | – |
| 3 kg. | – | – | – | – |
| **Pale Dry Malt Extract** | | | | |
| 0.75 lb. | – | – | – | – |
| 0.34 kg. | – | – | – | – |

## HOPPING SCHEDULE

| | | | | |
|---|---|---|---|---|
| **Bittering Hops** | | | | |
| 2.25-3.25 oz. | 1-1.5 oz. | 6.2-9.3 oz. | 1-1.5 oz. | 6.2-9.3 oz. |
| 64-92 gm. | 28.4-42.5 gm. | 176-264 gm. | 28.4-42.5 gm. | 176-264 gm. |
| 11.25-13 AAU | 5-6 AAU | 31-37.2 AAU | 5-6 AAU | 31-37.2 AAU |
| **Flavoring Hops** | | | | |
| 1.75-2.5 oz. | 0.75-1.125 oz. | 4.7-7 oz. | 0.75-1.125 oz. | 4.7-7 oz. |
| 50-71 gm. | 21-32 gm. | 133-198 gm. | 21-32 gm. | 133-198 gm. |
| **Aroma Hops** | | | | |
| – | – | – | – | – |

# Appendix:
# Commercial Bocks

**Einbecker Ur-Bock Hell, Maibock.** These are, of course, the exemplars of the pale Bock style. They are more robust than some of the others, having more color and a higher hopping rate, both for bitterness and for flavor/aroma. It is no wonder that Martin Luther thrived on this beer.

**Paulaner Salvator.** Although this can be traced directly back through the brewery to the monastic days, the beer has undergone a gradual updating. The final gravity has dropped by more than 0.010 (2.5 °Plato) in the last century, with a corresponding increase in alcohol level. As a result, it has become drier and less filling. It has a rich, dark malt character that finishes long and lingering, with just background hop bitterness.

**Ayinger Celebrator and Weihnachtsbock.** The Ayinger brewery, dominating the tiny farming village of Aying southeast of Munich, produces some of the most distinctive dunkles Bocks. They are particularly rich and sweet, but the sweetness is balanced by a larger contribution of

Photo by Jay Dotson.

roasted malt. The result is a complex, elegant product of great depth. The Weihnachtsbock (Christmas Bock), introduced each year at the beginning of December, is a slightly stronger version of the Celebrator, with six months of lagering.

**Ayinger Maibock.** One of the palest of the helles Bock beers, and also very lightly hopped, this beer is very delicate in spite of its strength. The brewmaster is producing a straightforward product that focuses entirely on the malt character, which arises from the on-premises maltings and local barley.

**Andechs Bergbock Helles Bock and Dunkles Doppelbock.** The Andechs monastery, located south of Munich, produces some of the most intensely malty products in the world. The brothers are secretive and only by reverse engineering (detailed chemical analysis of the product)[16,17] is it possible to even talk about attenuation and hopping rate. The helles is deceivingly pale, being a light gold, but the maltiness immediately overcomes this first impression. The Doppelbock, one of the lighter of the dunkles beers, has a very low attenuation and is very rich and sating.

**Doppelspaten Optimator.** Spaten's Optimator is a direct response to the Salvator classic. Optimator is made from a higher portion of black malts, and this shows through in its dry finish in spite of its lower attenuation than Salvator. The black malt is also employed as a substitute for hop bitterness, as Optimator has one of the lowest hopping rates.

**EKU Kulminator and EKU 28.** EKU (Erste Kulmbacher Actienbrauerei) is the largest brewery in the town of Kulmbach, nestled in a fold of the Franconian hills. Its brewery is housed in a fantastic modern sculpture of a building in the center of the city. Its beers are no less distinctive than the brewery's architecture. Kulminator is a wonderfully rich dunkles Doppelbock, with a surprisingly high final gravity that harks

Photo by Jay Dotson.

back to Doppelbocks of the last century. EKU 28, so named for its guaranteed original gravity of at least 1.112 (28 °Plato), produces a beer that is one of the two or three strongest. It also has, by far, the highest quantity of unfermented residual malt sugars. This makes the beer extremely filling, and requires that it be sipped slowly.

**Mönchshof Kloster Bock Dunkel.** This brewery, also located in Kulmbach, is rightly famous for its *schwartzbier* (black beer), which might be thought of as the lager world's answer to stout. Their Klosterbock is an extension of this style into Bock strength territory. The more strident flavor of the black malt is blended wonderfully

Photo by Jay Dotson.

with the usual large, rich body of the Bock beer. The combination is a winning one.

**Kulmbacher Reichelbräu G'frorns Eisbock.** The third of four breweries in Kulmbach, Reichelbräu along with Mönchshof and Sandlerbräu have common ownership, although they all maintain separate and distinct product lines. Reichelbräu claims to be the oldest brewery in the city, through a series of mergers and takeovers. Their specialty, Bayrische G'frorns (Bavarian Frozen) is an Eisbock — a beer that is concentrated by freeze distillation. It has an effective original gravity of 1.096 (24 °Plato). It is smooth, and as much as is possible for a beer of this strength, drinkable. Its richness and high alcohol do not diminish the dark malt character of the beer, and the higher level of carbonation also helps to lighten its immense body.

**Aass Bock.** The very pretty Bryggeri Aass built on the shores of the Drammen Fjord southwest of Olso, Norway, produces a double-decoction dunkles Bock which begins with a half hour infusion before the malt is run through the brewery's wet mill. The resulting beer is redolent with caramel flavors and aromas and a bit of candy sweetness. It is sating beyond its original gravity, which is fortunate when one considers the extreme alcohol taxes in effect in Norway, where a normal Pilsener can cost more than six dollars in a restaurant.

**Moretti La Rossa.** This Doppelbock strength beer (18 °Plato, the neck wrapper proclaims) is a rich and very warming product from Italy. Its unusual color is in the amber range, in between the paler helles varieties and the dunkles.

# Glossary

**adjunct.** Any unmalted grain or other fermentable ingredient added to the mash.

**aeration.** The action of introducing air to the wort at various stages of the brewing process.

**airlock.** (see fermentation lock)

**airspace.** (see ullage)

**alcohol by volume (v/v).** The percentage of volume of alcohol per volume of beer. To calculate the approximate volumetric alcohol content, subtract the terminal gravity from the original gravity and divide the result by 75. For example: $1.050 - 1.012 = .038 / 0.0075 = 5\%$ v/v.

**alcohol by weight (w/v).** The percentage weight of alcohol per volume of beer. For example: 3.2% alcohol by weight = 3.2 grams of alcohol per 100 centiliters of beer. Alcohol by weight can be converted to alcohol by volume by multiplying by 0.795.

**aldehyde.** A contraction of alcohol dehydrogenate. These compounds are characterized as oxidized alcohols, with a terminal CHO group.

**ale.** 1. Historically, an unhopped malt beverage; 2. Now a generic term for hopped beers produced by top fermentation, as opposed to lagers, which are produced by bottom fermentation.

**all-extract beer.** A beer made with only malt extract as opposed to one made from barley, or a combination of malt extract and barley.

**all-grain beer.** A beer made with only malted barley as opposed to one made from malt extract, or from malt extract and malted barley.

**all-malt beer.** A beer made with only barley malt with no adjuncts or refined sugars.

**alpha acid.** A soft resin in hop cones. When boiled, alpha acids are converted to iso-alpha-acids, which account for 60 percent of a beer's bitterness.

**alpha-acid unit.** A measurement of the potential bitterness of hops, expressed by their percentage of alpha acid. Low = 2 to 4%, medium = 5 to 7%, high = 8 to 12%. Abbrev: A.A.U.

**alt.** The german word for old. This is an old-fashioned, top-fermenting style of beer that undergoes a cold lagering for maturation.

**amino acids.** The building blocks of proteins. Essential components of wort, required for adequate yeast growth.

**attenuation.** The reduction in the wort's specific gravity caused by the transformation of sugars into alcohol and carbon-dioxide gas.

**Balling.** A saccharometer invented by Carl Joseph Napoleon Balling in 1843. It is calibrated for 63.5 degrees F (17.5 degrees C), and graduated in grams per hundred, giving a direct reading of the percentage of extract by weight per 100 grams solution. For example: 10 °B = 10 grams of sugar per 100 grams of wort.

**blow-by (blow-off).** A single-stage homebrewing fermentation method in which a plastic tube is fitted into the mouth of a carboy, with the other end submerged in a pail of sterile water. Unwanted residues and carbon dioxide are expelled through the tube, while air is prevented from coming into contact with the fermenting beer, thus avoiding contamination.

**carbonation.** The process of introducing carbon-dioxide gas into a liquid by: 1. injecting the finished beer with carbon dioxide; 2. adding young fermenting beer to finished beer for a renewed fermentation (kraeusening); 3. priming (adding sugar) to fermented wort prior to bottling, creating a secondary fermentation in the bottle; 4. finishing fermentation under pressure.

**carboy.** A large glass, plastic or earthenware bottle.

**chill haze.** Haziness caused by protein and tannin during the secondary fermentation.

**dimethyl sulfide (DMS).** An important sulfur-carrying compound originating in malt. Adds a crisp, "lager-like" character at low levels and corn or cabbage flavors at high levels.

**dry hopping.** The addition of hops to the primary fermenter, the secondary fermenter, or to casked beer to add aroma and hop character to the finished beer without adding significant bitterness.

**dry malt.** Malt extract in powdered form.

**EBC (European Brewery Convention).** (See SRM.)

**ester.** A class of organic compounds created from the reaction of an alcohol and an organic acid. These tend to have fruity aromas and are detectable at low concentrations.

**extract.** The amount of dissolved materials in the wort after mashing and lautering malted barley and/or malt adjuncts such as corn and rice.

**fermentation lock.** A one-way valve, which allows carbon-dioxide gas to escape from the fermenter while excluding contaminants.

**final specific gravity.** The specific gravity of a beer when fermentation is complete.

**fining.** The process of adding clarifying agents to beer during secondary fermentation to precipitate suspended matter.

**flocculation.** The behavior of yeast cells joining into masses and settling out toward the end of fermentation.

**homebrewers bittering units.** A formula invented by the American Homebrewers Association to measure bitterness of beer. Example: 1.5 ounces of hops at 10 percent alpha acid for five gallons: 1.5 x 10 = 15 HBU per five gallons.

**hop pellets.** Finely powdered hop cones compressed into tablets. Hop pellets are 20 to 30 percent more bitter by weight than the same variety in loose form.

**hydrometer.** A glass instrument used to measure the specific gravity of liquids as compared to water, consisting of a graduated stem resting on a weighed float.

**International Bitterness Unit.** This is an empirical quantity which was originally designed to measure the concentration of iso-alpha-acids in milligrams per liter (parts per million). Most procedures will also measure a small amount of uncharacterized soft resins so IBUs are generally 5 to 10% higher than iso-alpha acid concentrations.

**isinglass.** A gelatinous substance made from the swim bladder of certain fish and added to beer as a fining agent.

**kraeusen.** (n.) The rocky head of foam which appears on the surface of the wort during fermentation. (v.) To add fermenting wort to fermented beer to induce carbonation through a secondary fermentation.

**lager.** (n.) A generic term for any bottom-fermented beer. Lager brewing is now the predominant brewing method worldwide except in Britain where top fermented ales dominate. (v.) To store beer at near-zero temperatures in order to precipitate yeast cells and proteins and improve taste.

**lauter tun.** A vessel in which the mash settles and the grains are removed from the sweet wort through a straining process. It has a false, slotted bottom and spigot.

**liquefaction.** The process by which alpha-amylase enzymes degrade soluble starch into dextrin.

**malt.** Barley that has been steeped in water, germinated, then dried in kilns. This process converts insoluble starchs to soluble substances and sugars.

**malt extract.** A thick syrup or dry powder prepared from malt.

**mashing.** Mixing ground malt with water to extract the fermentables, degrade haze-forming proteins and convert grain starches to fermentable sugars and nonfermentable carbohydrates.

**modification.** 1. The physical and chemical changes in barley as a result of malting. 2. The degree to which these changes have occured, as determined by the growth of the acrospire.

**original gravity.** The specific gravity of wort previous to fermentation. A measure of the total amount of dissolved solids in wort.

**pH.** A measure of acidity or alkalinity of a solution, usually on a scale of one to fourteen, where seven is neutral.

**Plato.** A saccharometer that expresses specific gravity as extract weight in a one-hundred-gram solution at 68 degrees F (20 degrees C). A revised, more accurate version of Balling, developed by Dr. Plato.

**polyphenol.** Complexes of phenolic compounds involved in chill haze formation and oxidative staling.

**primary fermentation.** The first stage of fermentation, during which most fermentable sugars are converted to ethyl alcohol and carbon dioxide.

**priming sugar.** A small amount of corn, malt, or cane sugar added to bulk beer prior to racking or at bottling, to induce a new fermentation and create carbonation.

**racking.** The process of transferring beer from one container to another, especially into the final package (bottles, kegs, etc.).

**saccharification.** The naturally occurring process in which malt starch is converted into fermentable sugars, primarily maltose.

**saccharometer.** An instrument that determines the sugar concentration of a solution by measuring the specific gravity.

**secondary fermentation.** 1. The second, slower stage of fermentation, lasting from a few weeks to many months depending on the type of beer. 2. A fermentation occuring in bottles or casks and initiated by priming or by adding yeast.

**sparging.** Spraying the spent grains in the mash with hot water to retrieve the remaining malt sugar.

**specific gravity.** A measure of a substance's density as compared to that of water, which is given the value of 1.000 at 39.2 degrees F (4 degrees C). Specific gravity has no accompanying units, because it is expressed as a ratio.

**SRM (Standard Reference Method) and EBC (European Brewery Convention).** Two different analytical methods of describing color developed by comparing color samples. Degrees SRM, approximately equivalent to degrees Lovibond, are used by the ASBC (American Society of Brewing Chemists) while degrees EBC are European units. The following equations show approximate conversions:

Bock

(°EBC) = 2.65 x (°Lovibond) – 1.2

(°Lovibond) = 0.377 x (°EBC) + 0.45

**starter.** A batch of fermenting yeast, added to the wort to initiate fermentation.

**strike temperature.** The initial temperature of the water when the malted barley is added to it to create the mash.

**tannin.** (See polyphenol.)

**trub.** Suspended particles resulting from the precipitation of proteins, hop oils, and tannins during boiling and cooling stages of brewing.

**ullage.** The empty space between a liquid and the top of its container. Also called airspace or headspace.

**v/v.** (See alcohol by volume.)

**w/v.** (See alcohol by weight.)

**water hardness.** The degree of dissolved minerals in water.

**wort.** The mixture that results from mashing the malt and boiling the hops, before it is fermented into beer.

# Bibliography

## LISTED BY AUTHOR

Arnold, John P. *Origin and History of Beer and Brewing.* Chicago Ill.: Alumni Association of the Wahl-Henius Institute of Fermentology, 1911. (6)

*Brewer's Technical Review.* March 1936, (Vol. 11, No. 3). Chicago, Ill.: Siebel Publishing Co. (3)

*Brewer's Technical Review.* March 1937, (Vol. 12, No. 3). Chicago, Ill.: Siebel Publishing Co. (4)

Briggs, D.E.; Hough, J.S.; Stevens, R.; and Young, T.W. *Malting and Brewing Science.* 2nd ed., rev. London, United Kingdom: Chapman and Hall, 1971. (23)

Brischke, Georg W.A. *Betriebsstörungen bei der Bierbereitung.* Nürnberg, Germany: Verlag Hans Carl, 1954. (26)

Broderick, Harold M., ed. *The Practical Brewer.* 2nd ed., rev. Madison, Wis.: Master Brewers Association of the Americas, 1977. (25)

*Consumer Reports.* January 1990, (Vol. 55, No. 1). Yonkers, N.Y.: Consumers Union of the United States, Inc. (32)

De Clerck, Jean. *A Textbook of Brewing.* 2 vols. Translated by Kathleen Barton-Wright. London, United Kingdom: Chapman & Hall Ltd., 1957. (37)

Ecimovich III, Victor. "Bock." *zymurgy*, Special Issue 1991, (Vol. 14, No. 4): 29-30. (34)

Eckhardt, Fred. *The Essentials of Beer Style.* Portland, Ore.: Fred Eckhardt Associates, 1989. (1)

Fink, Dan. "Brew News." *zymurgy*, Winter 1990, (Vol 13, No. 5): 15-19. (43)

Fink, Dan. "Brew News." *zymurgy*, Summer 1991, (Vol 14, No. 2): 14-17. (44)

Fix, Dr. George. *Principles of Brewing Science.* Boulder, Colo.: Brewers Publications, 1989. (22)

Fix, Dr. George and Laurie. *Vienna, Märzen, Oktoberfest.* Classic Beer Style Series. Boulder, Colo.: Brewers Publications, 1991. (51)

Fix, Dr. George. "The Detriments of Hot Side Aeration." *zymurgy*, Winter 1992, (Vol. 15, No. 5): 32-40. (40)

Fix, Dr. George. "Some Practical Observations Concerning Belgium Malts." *Brewing Techniques.* (Vol. 1, No. 1), 1993. (49)

*400 Jarhe Hofbräuhaus München 1589-1989.* Munich, Germany: Carl Gerber Verlag GmbH, 1989. (11)

Gerlach, Wolfgang; Gutmann, Hermann; Hassenkamp, Michael; Udo, Moll; and Widmann, Werner A. *Das deutsche Bier.* Hamburg, Germany: HB Verlag, 1984. (13)

Gordon, Dan. "German Beer." In *Beer and Brewing, Vol. 10*, edited by Tracy Loyson. Boulder, Colo.: Brewers Publications, 1990. (50)

Guinard, Jean-Xavier. *Lambic.* Classic Beer Style Series. Boulder, Colo.: Brewers Publications, 1990. (24)

Hajek, Th. "Bock- oder Doppelbockbiere." *Die Brauwelt,* June 14, 1951, (Vol. 24): 503. (15)

Hauser, Dr. A. "Bedeutung und Herkunft des Bockbieres." *Schweizer Brauerei-Rundschau,* May 1962, (Vol. 73, No. 5): 79-80. (10)

Hoffman, M. *5000 Jahre Bier.* Nürnberg, Germany: Verlag Hans Carl, 1956. (12)

Jackson, Michael. *The New World Guide To Beer.* Philadelphia, Pa.: Running Press Book Publishers, 1988. (7)

Lewis, Michael J.; Robertson, Ian C.; and Dankers, Stephan U. "Proteolysis in the Protein Rest of Mashing— An Appraisal." *MBAA Technical Quarterly,* 1992, (Vol. 29, No. 4): 117-121. (48)

Line, Dave. *The Big Book Of Brewing.* Andover, Hants., United Kingdom: The Amateur Winemaker, 1974. (29)

Lodahl, Martin A. "Malt Extracts: Cause for Caution." *Brewing Techniques.* (Vol. 1, No. 2), 1993. (45)

Lübers, Dr. Ing. habil. Heinrich. *Die Wissenschaftlichen Grundlagen von Mälzerei und Brauerei.* Nürnberg, Germany: Verlag Hans Carl, 1956. (28)

Miller, Dave. *The Complete Handbook of Home Brewing.* Pownal, Vt.: Storey Communications, Inc., 1988. (35)

Miller, Dave. "Recipe Formulation: Experimenting with Munich Malt." In *Beer and Brewing, Vol. 10,* edited by Tracy Loysen. Boulder, Colo.: Brewers Publications, 1990. (30)

Mitterwieser, Dr. Alios. "Geschictes über Maibock, Salvator, Weiß- und Märzenbier." *Das Bayerland,* September 1927, (Vol. 37, No. 17): 515-517. (19)

Morris, Rodney. "Yeast Quality and Fermentation Conditions." In *Brew Free or Die, Beer and Brewing, Vol. 11,* edited by Tracy Loysen. Boulder, Colo.: Brewers Publications, 1991. (52)

Narziß, Dr. Ludwig. "Die Technologie der Malzbereitung." In *Die Bierbrauerei.* Vol. 1. 6th ed., rev. Stuttgart, Germany: Ferdinand Enke Verlag, 1976. (41)

Narziß, Dr. Ludwig. *Abriß der Bierbrauerei.* 5th ed., rev. Stuttgart, Germany: Ferdinand Enke Verlag, 1986. (27)

Narziß, Dr. Ludwig. "Die Technologie der Würzebereitung." In *Die Bierbrauerei.* Vol. 2. 7th ed., rev. Stuttgart, Germany: Ferdinand Enke Verlag, 1992. (39)

Noonan, Gregory J. *Brewing Lager Beer.* Boulder, Colo.: Brewers Publications: 1986. (36)

Noonan, Gregory J. "Water Workshop." In *Brew Free or Die, Beer and Brewing, Vol. 11*, edited by Tracy Loysen. Boulder, Colo.: Brewers Publications, 1991. (31)

Noonan, Gregory J. *Scotch Ale.* Classic Beer Styles Series. Boulder, Colo.: Brewers Publications: 1993. (53)

*100 Years of Brewing, A Supplement to the Western Brewer.* Chicago, Ill., and New York, N.Y.: H.S. Rich and Sons, 1903. (14)

Paik, J.; Low, N.H.; and Ingledew, W.M. "Malt Extract: Relationship of Chemical Composition to Fermentability." *Journal of the American Society of Brewing Chemists*, 1991, (Vol. 49). (42)

Piendl, Professor Dr. Anton. "500 Biere aus Aller Welt." *Brauindustrie*, 1985, (Vol. 70, No. 1): 59-67. (16)

Piendl, Professor Dr. Anton. "Biere aus Aller Welt." *Brauindustrie*, 1985, (Vol. 70, No. 20): 1881-1894. (17)

Rager, Jackie. "Calculating Hop Bitterness in Beer." *zymurgy*, Special Issue 1990, (Vol. 13, No. 4): 53-54. (46)

Reed, Gerald and Nagodawithana, Tilak W. *Yeast Technology.* 2nd ed., rev. New York, N.Y.: Van Norstrand Reinhold, 1991. (47)

Sample Brew Log for Batch 331. Stephansquelle pale Doppelbock beer of the Bayrische Staatsbrauerei. Weihenstephan, June 1984. (20)

Thausing, Julius E. *The Theory and Practice of the Preparation of Malt and the Fabrication of Beer.* Philadelphia, Pa.: Henry Carey Baird & Co., 1882. (18)

von Wagner, Ladislaus. *Handbuch der Bierbrauerei Nach dem Heutigen Standpunkte der Theorie und Praxis.* 2 vols. Weimar, Germany: Bernhard Friedrich Voigt, 1877. (19)

Wahl, Robert, and Henius, Max. *The American Handy Book of the Brewing, Malting and Auxiliary Trades.* 3rd ed., rev. Chicago, Ill.: Wahl-Henius Institute, 1908. (2)

Walther, Erwin. "Welcher Bock war's der den Ritter umstieß?" *Bier-Ein Welt Report*, May 1979, (Vol. 5, No. 24): 24. (8)

Warner, Eric. *German Wheat Beer.* Classic Beer Style Series. Boulder, Colo.: Brewers Publications, 1992. (5)

Weast, Dr. Robert, ed. *Handbook of Chemistry and Physics.* 53rd ed., rev. Cleveland, Ohio: Chemical Rubber Co. Press, 1972-1973. (33)

Weinfurtner, Von F.; Wullinger, F.; and Piendl, A. "Die Zuckerbildung in den Maischen, der Vorderwürze und den Nachgüßen bei der Herstellung von verschiedenen Biersorten: von dunklem Starkbier." *Brauwelt*, September 1965, (Vol. 105, No. 74/75): 1361-1370. (38)

Wild, Josef. *Aus Meinem Leben und Schaffen in München und Berlin.* Berlin, Germany: Institut für Gärungsgewerbe, 1937. (21)

## LISTED BY NUMBER

1.   Eckhardt, Fred. *The Essentials of Beer Style.* Portland, Ore.: Fred Eckhardt Associates, 1989.

2. Wahl, Robert, and Henius, Max. *The American Handy Book of the Brewing, Malting and Auxiliary Trades.* 3rd ed., rev. Chicago, Ill.: Wahl-Henius Institute, 1908.

*3. Brewer's Technical Review.* March 1936, (Vol. 11, No. 3). Chicago, Ill.: Siebel Publishing Co.

*4. Brewer's Technical Review.* March 1937, (Vol. 12, No. 3). Chicago, Ill.: Siebel Publishing Co.

5. Warner, Eric. *German Wheat Beer.* Classic Beer Style Series. Boulder, Colo.: Brewers Publications, 1992.

6. Arnold, John P. *Origin and History of Beer and Brewing.* Chicago Ill.: Alumni Association of the Wahl-Henius Institute of Fermentology, 1911.

7. Jackson, Michael. *The New World Guide To Beer.* Philadelphia, Pa.: Running Press Book Publishers, 1988.

8. Walther, Erwin. "Welcher Bock war's der den Ritter umstieß?" *Bier-Ein Welt Report,* May 1979, (Vol. 5, No. 24): 24.

9. Mitterwieser, Dr. Alios. "Geschictes über Maibock, Salvator, Weiß- und Märzenbier." *Das Bayerland,* September 1927, (Vol. 37, No. 17): 515-517.

10. Hauser, Dr. A. "Bedeutung und Herkunft des Bockbieres." *Schweizer Brauerei-Rundschau,* May 1962, (Vol. 73, No. 5): 79-80.

11. *400 Jarhe Hofbräuhaus München 1589-1989.* Munich, Germany: Carl Gerber Verlag GmbH, 1989.

_Bock_

12. Hoffman, M. *5000 Jahre Bier*. Nürnberg, Germany: Verlag Hans Carl, 1956.

13. Gerlach, Wolfgang; Gutmann, Hermann; Hassenkamp, Michael; Udo, Moll; and Widmann, Werner A. *Das deutsche Bier*. Hamburg, Germany: HB Verlag, 1984.

14. *100 Years of Brewing, A Supplement to the Western Brewer*. Chicago, Ill. and New York, N.Y.: H.S. Rich and Sons, 1903.

15. Hajek, Th. "Bock- oder Doppelbockbiere." *Die Brauwelt*, June 14, 1951, (Vol. 24): 503.

16. Piendl, Professor Dr. Anton. "500 Biere aus Aller Welt." *Brauindustrie*, 1985, (Vol. 70, No. 1): 59-67.

17. Piendl, Professor Dr. Anton. "Biere aus Aller Welt." *Brauindustrie*, 1985, (Vol. 70, No. 20): 1881-1894.

18. Thausing, Julius E. *The Theory and Practice of the Preparation of Malt and the Fabrication of Beer*. Philadelphia, Pa.: Henry Carey Baird & Co., 1882.

19. von Wagner, Ladislaus. *Handbuch der Bierbrauerei Nach dem Heutigen Standpunkte der Theorie und Praxis*. 2 vols. Weimar, Germany: Bernhard Friedrich Voigt, 1877.

20. Sample Brew Log for Batch 331. Stephansquelle pale Doppelbock beer of the Bayrische Staatsbrauerei. Weihenstephan, June 1984.

21. Wild, Josef. *Aus Meinem Leben und Schaffen in Munchen und Berlin*. Berlin, Germany: Institut für Gärungsgewerbe, 1937.

22. Fix, Dr. George. *Principles of Brewing Science*. Boulder, Colo.: Brewers Publications, 1989.

23. Briggs, D.E.; Hough, J.S.; Stevens, R.; and Young, T.W. *Malting and Brewing Science*. 2nd ed., rev. London, United Kingdom: Chapman and Hall, 1971.

24. Guinard, Jean-Xavier. *Lambic*. Classic Beer Styles Series. Boulder, Colo.: Brewers Publications, 1990.

25. Broderick, Harold M., ed. *The Practical Brewer*. 2nd ed., rev. Madison, Wis.: Master Brewers Association of the Americas, 1977.

26. Brischke, Georg W.A. *Betriebsstörungen bei der Bierbereitung*. Nürnberg, Germany: Verlag Hans Carl, 1954.

27. Narziß, Dr. Ludwig. *Abriß der Bierbrauerei*. 5th ed., rev. Stuttgart, Germany: Ferdinand Enke Verlag, 1986.

28. Lübers, Dr. Ing. habil. Heinrich. *Die Wissenschaftlichen Grundlagen von Mälzerei und Brauerei*. Nürnberg, Germany: Verlag Hans Carl, 1956.

29. Line, Dave. *The Big Book Of Brewing*. Andover, Hants., United Kingdom: The Amateur Winemaker, 1974.

30. Miller, Dave. "Recipe Formulation: Experimenting with Munich Malt." In *Beer and Brewing, Vol. 10*, edited by Tracy Loysen. Boulder, Colo.: Brewers Publications, 1990.

31. Noonan, Gregory J. "Water Workshop." In *Brew Free or Die, Beer and Brewing, Vol. 11*, edited by Tracy Loysen. Boulder, Colo.: Brewers Publications, 1991.

32. *Consumer Reports.* January 1990, (Vol. 55, No. 1). Yonkers, N.Y.: Consumers Union of the United States, Inc.

33. Weast, Dr. Robert, ed. *Handbook of Chemistry and Physics.* 53rd ed., rev. Cleveland, Ohio: Chemical Rubber Co. Press, 1972-1973.

34. Ecimovich III, Victor. "Bock." *zymurgy,* Special Issue 1991, (Vol. 14, No. 4): 29-30.

35. Miller, Dave. *The Complete Handbook of Home Brewing.* Pownal, Vt.: Storey Communications, Inc., 1988.

36. Noonan, Gregory J. *Brewing Lager Beer.* Boulder, Colo.: Brewers Publications: 1986.

37. De Clerck, Jean. *A Textbook of Brewing.* 2 vols. Translated by Kathleen Barton-Wright. London, United Kingdom: Chapman & Hall Ltd., 1957.

38. Weinfurtner, Von F.; Wullinger, F.; and Piendl, A. "Die Zuckerbildung in den Maischen, der Vorderwürze und den Nachgüßen bei der Herstellung von verschiedenen Biersorten: von dunklem Starkbier." *Brauwelt,* September 1965, (Vol. 105, No. 74/75): 1361-1370.

39. Narziß, Dr. Ludwig. "Die Technologie der Würzebereitung." In *Die Bierbrauerei.* Vol. 2. 7th ed., rev. Stuttgart, Germany: Ferdinand Enke Verlag, 1992.

40. Fix, Dr. George. "The Detriments of Hot Side Aeration." *zymurgy,* Winter 1992, (Vol. 15, No. 5): 32-40.

41. Narziß, Dr. Ludwig. "Die Technologie der Malzbereitung." In *Die Bierbrauerei*. Vol. 1. 6th ed., rev. Stuttgart, Germany: Ferdinand Enke Verlag, 1976.

42. Paik, J.; Low, N.H.; and Ingledew, W.M. "Malt Extract: Relationship of Chemical Composition to Fermentability." *Journal of the American Society of Brewing Chemists*, 1991, (Vol. 49).

43. Fink, Dan. "Brew News." *zymurgy*, Winter 1990, (Vol 13, No. 5): 15-19.

44. Fink, Dan. "Brew News." *zymurgy*, Summer 1991, (Vol 14, No. 2): 14-17.

45. Lodahl, Martin A. "Malt Extracts: Cause for Caution." *Brewing Techniques*. (Vol. 1, No. 2), 1993.

46. Rager, Jackie. "Calculating Hop Bitterness in Beer." *zymurgy*, Special Issue 1990, (Vol. 13, No. 4): 53-54.

47. Reed, Gerald and Nagodawithana, Tilak W. *Yeast Technology*. 2nd ed., rev. New York, N.Y.: Van Norstrand Reinhold, 1991.

48. Lewis, Michael J.; Robertson, Ian C.; and Dankers, Stephan U. "Proteolysis in the Protein Rest of Mashing— An Appraisal." *MBAA Technical Quarterly*, 1992, (Vol. 29, No. 4): 117-121.

49. Fix, Dr. George. "Some Practical Observations Concerning Belgium Malts." *Brewing Techniques*. (Vol. 1, No. 1), 1993.

50. Gordon, Dan. "German Beer." In *Beer and Brewing, Vol. 10*, edited by Tracy Loyson. Boulder, Colo.: Brewers Publications, 1990.

51. Fix, Dr. George and Laurie. *Vienna, Märzen, Oktoberfest.* Classic Beer Styles Series. Boulder, Colo.: Brewers Publications, 1991.

52. Morris, Rodney. "Yeast Quality and Fermentation Conditions." In *Brew Free or Die, Beer and Brewing, Vol. 11,* edited by Tracy Loysen. Boulder, Colo.: Brewers Publications, 1991.

53. Noonan, Gregory J. *Scotch Ale.* Classic Beer Styles Series. Boulder, Colo.: Brewers Publications: 1993.

# Index

# HOMEBREWER?

Join the thousands of American Homebrewers Association members who read **zymurgy** — the magazine for homebrewers and beer lovers.

Every issue of **zymurgy** is full of tips, techniques, new recipes, new products, equipment and ingredient reviews, beer news, technical articles — the whole world of homebrewing. PLUS, the AHA brings members the National Homebrewers Conference, the National Homebrew Competition, the Beer Judge Certification Program, the Homebrew Club Network, periodic discounts on books from Brewers Publications and much, much more.

## Photocopy and mail this coupon today to join the AHA or call now for credit card orders, (303) 546-6514.

Name

Address

City       State/Province

Zip/Postal Code       Country

Phone

☐ Enclosed is $29 for one full year.
Canadian memberships are $34 US, Foreign memberships are $44 US.

☐ Please charge my credit card ☐ Visa ☐ MC

Card No.   —   —   —     Exp. Date

Signature

Make check to: American Homebrewers Association, PO Box 1510, Boulder, CO 80306 USA
Offer valid until 12/31/95.     Prices subject to change.     BOCK

# BOOKS for Brewers and Beer Lovers

## Order Now ... Your Brew Will Thank You!

These books offered by Brewers Publications are some of the most sought after reference tools for homebrewers and professional brewers alike. Filled with tips, techniques, recipes and history, these books will help you expand your brewing horizons. Let the world's foremost brewers help you as you brew. So whatever your brewing level or interest, Brewers Publications has the information necessary for you to brew the best beer in the world — your beer.

- - - - - - - - - - - - - - - - - - - - - - - - - - - - - - - - -

## Please send me more free information on the following: (check all that apply)

◊ Merchandise & Book Catalog
◊ American Homebrewers Association
◊ Institute for Brewing Studies
◊ Great American Beer Festival℠

### Ship to:

Name
_____

Address
_____

City _____ State/Province _____

Zip/Postal Code _____ Country _____

Daytime Phone ( )
_____

Please use the following in conjunction with an order form when ordering books from Brewers Publications.

### Payment Method

◊ Check or Money Order Enclosed (Payable to the Association of Brewers)
◊ Visa ◊ MasterCard

Card Number ___ – ___ – ___ Expiration Date _____

Name on Card _____ Signature _____

**Brewers Publications, PO Box 1679, Boulder, CO 80306-1679, (303) 546-6514, FAX (303) 447-2825.**

# BREWERS PUBLICATIONS ORDER FORM

## PROFESSIONAL BREWING BOOKS

| QTY. | TITLE | STOCK # | PRICE | EXT. PRICE |
|------|-------|---------|-------|------------|
| _____ | Brewery Planner | 500 | 80.00 | _____ |
| _____ | North American Brewers Resource Directory | 504 | 80.00 | _____ |
| _____ | Principles of Brewing Science | 463 | 29.95 | _____ |

### THE BREWERY OPERATIONS SERIES
### from Micro and Pubbrewers Conferences

| QTY. | TITLE | STOCK # | PRICE | EXT. PRICE |
|------|-------|---------|-------|------------|
| _____ | Volume 4, 1987 Conference | 534 | 25.95 | _____ |
| _____ | Volume 5, 1988 Conference | 535 | 25.95 | _____ |
| _____ | Volume 6, 1989 Conference | 536 | 25.95 | _____ |
| _____ | Volume 7, 1990 Conference | 537 | 25.95 | _____ |
| _____ | Volume 8, 1991 Conference, Brewing Under Adversity | 538 | 25.95 | _____ |
| _____ | Volume 9, 1992 Conference, Quality Brewing — Share the Experience | 539 | 25.95 | _____ |

## CLASSIC BEER STYLE SERIES

| QTY. | TITLE | STOCK # | PRICE | EXT. PRICE |
|------|-------|---------|-------|------------|
| _____ | Pale Ale | 401 | 11.95 | _____ |
| _____ | Continental Pilsener | 402 | 11.95 | _____ |
| _____ | Lambic | 403 | 11.95 | _____ |
| _____ | Vienna, Märzen, Oktoberfest | 404 | 11.95 | _____ |
| _____ | Porter | 405 | 11.95 | _____ |
| _____ | Belgian Ale | 406 | 11.95 | _____ |
| _____ | German Wheat Beer | 407 | 11.95 | _____ |
| _____ | Scotch Ale | 408 | 11.95 | _____ |
| _____ | Bock | 409 | 11.95 | _____ |

## BEER AND BREWING SERIES, for homebrewers and beer enthusiasts,
## from National Homebrewers Conferences

| QTY. | TITLE | STOCK # | PRICE | EXT. PRICE |
|------|-------|---------|-------|------------|
| _____ | Volume 8, 1988 Conference | 448 | 21.95 | _____ |
| _____ | Volume 10, 1990 Conference | 450 | 21.95 | _____ |
| _____ | Volume 11, 1991 Conference, Brew Free Or Die! | 451 | 21.95 | _____ |
| _____ | Volume 12, 1992 Conference, Just Brew It! | 452 | 21.95 | _____ |

## GENERAL BEER AND BREWING INFORMATION

| QTY. | TITLE | STOCK # | PRICE | EXT. PRICE |
|------|-------|---------|-------|------------|
| _____ | Brewing Lager Beer | 460 | 14.95 | _____ |
| _____ | Brewing Mead | 461 | 11.95 | _____ |
| _____ | Dictionary of Beer and Brewing | 462 | 19.95 | _____ |
| _____ | Evaluating Beer | 465 | 25.95 | _____ |
| _____ | Great American Beer Cookbook | 466 | 24.95 | _____ |
| _____ | Winners Circle | 464 | 11.95 | _____ |

**SUBTOTAL** _____

Call or write for a free *Beer Enthusiast* catalog today.
Colo. Residents Add 3% Sales Tax _____
• U.S. funds only.
• All Brewers Publications books come with a money-back guarantee.
**P & H *** _____
* **Postage & Handling:** $4 for the first book ordered, plus $1 for each book thereafter. Canadian and foreign orders please add $5 for the first book and $2 for each book thereafter. Orders cannot be shipped without appropriate P&H.
**TOTAL** _____

Brewers Publications, PO Box 1679, Boulder, CO 80306-1679, (303) 546-6514, FAX (303) 447-2825.